IT BEGAN WITH A ROAR!

Dr. Harry Wegeforth and the San Diego Zoo's first elephant.

IT BEGAN WITH A

R·O·A·R!

The Beginning of the World-Famous San Diego Zoo

by Dr. Harry M. Wegeforth
and Neil Morgan

A Zoological Society of San Diego Publication

Dr. Harry M. Wegeforth
1882–1941

Harry Wegeforth must have been the only man in the world who learned to play a fife solely to keep a pet pigeon happy. He was nine then. Before he died, fifty years later in San Diego, he had traded pigeon for giraffe, gorilla, and gnu—and used his life to build a monument to man's love for animals at the San Diego Zoo.

The story of San Diego has been studded with the names of men who almost singlehandedly breathed life into the city. Among them, Dr. Harry Wegeforth took rank as a physician, a suave diplomat, a belligerent fighter—but most of all as the man who decided, amid derisive cries in 1916, that a leftover collection of animals on display for exposition crowds should become the nucleus of a zoo which would bring to San Diego the plaudits of the world. For the next twenty-five years, he headed the San Diego Zoo. Before he died in 1941, the Zoo that "Doctor Harry" built was being called one of the finest on earth.

He called the thousands of creatures in the Zoo his family. They were. For them, he defied politicians. He browbeat reluctant voters. He wooed wealthy donors. He "stole." He traveled, for them, into every part of the world, and also collected tickets at the gates of the Zoo. He powdered elephants white, tossed calomel into the mouth of an angry tiger, and stuffed a python with sausage from a meat grinder.

Just before he died, a newspaper reporter asked him why he had done it all.

"I like animals," he said, and that was all.

© 1990 by the Zoological Society of San Diego
Post Office Box 551
San Diego, California 92112

1990 edition revised
Cover art by Tim Reamer
Design by Thomas L. Scharf

First published in 1953
Paperback edition, revised, printed in 1969
Original typography and design for these editions by Richard B. Yale

Library of Congress Catalog Card Number: 90-071878

ISBN 0-911461-14-0

Copy editing by Mary Sekulovich
Indexing by William E. Becorest

Printed by Crest Offset Printing Company
National City, California
United States of America

Unless otherwise noted all photographs are from the collections of the Zoological Society of San Diego — Ron Garrison, photographic supervisor; Ken Kelly, photo technician; Edalee Orcutt Harwell, photo archivist.

All rights reserved. No part of this book may be reproduced or transmitted in any form or by any means, electronic or mechanical, including photocopying, recording, or by any information storage and retrieval system, without permission in writing from the publisher.

Name "ZOONOOZ" Reg. U.S. Pat. Office

Print number   5   4   3   2   1

CONTENTS

*Part One:
The Roar Begins
by Neil Morgan*

INTRODUCTION	11
FOREWORD	15
BACKYARD ZOO KEEPER	19
THIS WAS THE ROAR	23
MAN WITHOUT A TURTLE	29
ANIMAL LOBBYIST	32
DOCTOR TO A TIGER	40
PROMOTER AND SURGEON	46
ICE CREAM AND ELEPHANTS	53
TINAMOU TIZZY	56
HE TRAVELED FOR HIS "FAMILY"	60
THE "CHECK-IN"	66

CONTENTS

Part Two:
Stories of the Zoo
by Dr. Harry M. Wegeforth

A ZOO IS BORN	71
HOW TO KIDNAP AN ALLIGATOR	75
A HOME AT LAST	82
ELEPHANTS CAUSE HEADACHES	88
FROM PAPER PLANS TO REALITY	97
CRUSADING FOR ANTIVENIN	105
WE BUCK THE ANIMAL DEALERS	107
WE TURN SEAL HUNTERS	108
THE DIRECTOR PROBLEM IS SOLVED	113
NOW WE'RE LAND OWNERS	117
OF CAMELS, CHIMP, AND SNAKE	120
THE MID-TWENTIES: A ROARING TIME	124
INTO THE THIRTIES: FIGHT THROUGH TO SECURITY	129

CONTENTS

*Part Three:
The Roar Grows Louder
by Neil Morgan*

"DOCTOR HARRY'S" SHIP COMES IN	139
THE ZOO GEARS FOR WAR	140
THE NEW "FIRST TEAM"	150
ZOO, I LOVE YOU!	152
COMING OUT OF THE WAR	156
THE ZOO IS FAMED	160
BIG NEWS AND GORILLAS	163
THE ANIMALS ARE THE SHOW	166
EPILOGUE	171
INDEX	175

*To My Sons,
and All Who Helped
To Build the
San Diego Zoo*

RACHEL M. WEGEFORTH

INTRODUCTION

The following introduction appeared in the original 1953 edition of this book and is still one of the best descriptions of Dr. Harry Wegeforth's personality and work at the San Diego Zoo. Its author, Dr. Charles Schroeder, received his doctor of veterinary medicine degree from Washington State University in 1929 and was first hired as a veterinarian/pathologist at the Zoo in 1932. He later served as the Zoo's director from 1954 to 1972.

Are you interested in the behavior of living animals—3,500 of them [in 1990 this figure stands at approximately 3,800], the real thing on exhibit in the best possible environment—gorillas—elephant seals—koalas—Andean condors—and rare reptiles?

If you are, you will thoroughly enjoy this account of the founding and development of one of the world's great public institutions and the man who did it, prepared in a factual manner by a competent researcher and writer, aided by Mrs. Rachel Wegeforth. Doctor Harry's personal notes and the recollections of his many friends give the whole story warmth, but it is factual.

Service and devotion to the public good is too infrequently recognized. Whereas few of us have the opportunity or the privilege in our lifetime to achieve greatness, some have posthumous recognition. I have never met a man with Doctor Harry's animal-like persistence, or his tenacity of purpose to do the job and carry it to completion, come hell or high water.

If it is selfish to make personal sacrifices in fortune and energy for the sole reward of seeing a dream come to fruition, then Doctor Harry was a very selfish man. His goal was so clear, and the road was so narrow and straight that he would not permit any form of deviation no matter how sincere the volunteers, and he would not tolerate free riders. He had a plan to fit that bleak and rugged Balboa Park topography. He knew how to accomplish his end. He knew who would give the funds, the land, the animals. He had an inside track.

Little could he have foreseen a great depression and the formation, under the New Deal, of the Public Works Administration. But, he knew how to take advantage of this economic crisis to benefit the Zoo. The extensive WPA Zoo projects permitted early realization of many of his dreams, but he seemed to be racing continuously against time. The same energy applied to a private enterprise would have made him many times a millionaire. He had the happy faculty of enlisting the services of those in and out of his employ who had something he needed. He would never temporize and agreed that if you can't lick them, join them.

He planted the seed. We did his bidding without further interference. He knew how to pull the most out of everyone who would help, and you felt good about it. He gave you the authority to act in your position, as well as his support, and always his personal gratitude. The world has known no more stubborn or determined man. Like so many other great public builders, his critics are endless. If you knew him and worked with him, you couldn't think of lying down on the job. His enthusiasm was catching. You knew that when you were on Doctor Harry's side you were on the winning side, and felt secure.

Actually there was no formal plan. You learned how he thought, how he hoped to exhibit an animal, what the budget would permit, what the stop-gap or substitute would have to be; but you never lost sight of what he wanted done. As with many other successful builders, the impossible was just a little harder and took a little longer. He could enlist the cooperation of a camel.

He was a most unusual man. He shared his accomplishments, large or small, with all who contributed, even in a small way, to the success of the program—whether by use of their names or friends' names or funds, or the sweat of their brows. But he was the direct antagonist of credit seekers. In a modern industrial sense he was the perfect supervisor. He knew how to handle problems. He always let you know how you were getting along. He gave credit where it was due. He would let you in on the plans and especially those that would affect you. He knew how to make the best of each person's ability.

Research in nutritional, parasitic, and infectious diseases of wild animals held a high place on his agenda and led to the building of the Ellen Browning Scripps Biological Research Laboratories within the Zoo, and the establishment of the Scripps' graduate fellowships and publication of scientific papers. He had an interest in the frequent occurrence of gastric ulcers in sea mammals, mouth rot in snakes, protozoan diseases of birds, and allergic diseases of wild animals—but, in particular, diseases transmitted from animals to man. He was far ahead of his time in recognition of animals as carriers of infectious disease, but more especially the role primates and small mammals might play in human virus disease research.

Countless young men and women were inspired to become scientists under Doctor Harry's behind-the-scenes guidance: physicians, veterinarians, zoologists, and researchers in biological fields. Many have taken advantage of the Scripps' fellowships for graduate study.

We know that there will be many improvements in construction and services, new specimens, and novel exhibits that will all add to the relaxation, enjoyment, and education of San Diego children and their accompanying parents in the years to come.

INTRODUCTION

The Wegeforth ball has been rolling under the expert guidance of Belle Benchley, and who knows how far-reaching the San Diego influence will be!

Doctor Harry's close friendship with philanthropists, especially Captain G. Allan Hancock, led to many collection trips for the Zoo, museums, and other institutions—all adding to the international prestige of the San Diego Zoo. There were some shortcomings and frank disasters, but all were over-shadowed by his triumphs. It was a great day for San Diego when Doctor Harry chose our fair city for his home, and this posthumous award is long overdue.

Charles R. Schroeder, D.V.M.

FOREWORD

The first edition of this book appeared almost forty years ago, hardly more than a decade after the death of Dr. Harry Wegeforth. San Diego was a pleasant town then, one whose insularity went unchallenged.

Yet the zoo he had created, through the astonishing force of his lifelong passion for animals, was already talked of around America and Europe as the world's best zoo.

I was part of a restless generation who migrated westward, just as the man known as "Doctor Harry" had done in his youth. Many of us adopted San Diego, as he had a generation earlier, and began to echo the common sentiment that this was a place touched by destiny.

But the truth, it now seems to me, was that San Diego in those years was a transplanted Midwestern town beside the Pacific, with only rare bursts of the energies and vision that create a great city. About all that Americans knew of San Diego then were the rumors of a benevolent climate, its concentration of naval personnel and facilities, and its Zoo. The Almighty, to whom we attribute the climate and the natural harbor, seems responsible for two of these three claims to fame. True, San Diegans had already brought water and power across the desert to make life possible on this arid shore. They had staged two expositions in Balboa Park, at times when the economy of the city threatened to dry up like a desert waterhole and leave the place a ghost town. From the earlier exposition had come an appreciation of the city's natural harbor that helped lead the United States Navy to San Diego.

Still, only one of San Diego's three national notorieties was manmade, and that was Dr. Harry's Zoo. His pioneering in cageless animal display owed as much to San Diego's benign climate as it did to his skimpy budget. But the existence of the San Diego Zoo was a triumph of the obsession that drove this tenacious and persuasive surgeon throughout his life.

Four decades ago, as a young newspaperman, I spent evenings and weekends in the Zoo archives, preparing to write the bookends that Dr. Harry's widow Rachel asked me to provide, framing his own unpublished narrative about the beginnings of the Zoo. In rereading the portions of this book that I wrote then, I realize that, even before I understood the San Diego psyche, I was in awe of the deed that Dr. Harry had done. Now it seems even more extraordinary. One is not likely, even in today's more dynamic San Diego, to succeed at creating any remarkable institution. What it was like in the early years of this century is what this book is about.

Charlie Schroeder took over direction of the Zoo just after the first edition of this book was published and, for almost two decades, led it forward with great intellectual honesty, personal force, and persuasiveness not unlike those that set Dr. Harry apart. The next historian of the San Diego Zoo will be able to document the rare good fortune of the institution in its continuity of vision and interrelated styles of management. That historian may manage to draw a genealogical line of dynamism from Dr. Harry's grandstanding triumphs over the city hall bureaucracy to Charlie Schroeder's unflagging battle to build the Wild Animal Park as an animal breeding ground, on to the Zoo's extraordinary Center for Reproduction of Endangered Species, and even to Joan Embery's unlikely parade of San Diego Zoo animals into millions of homes as a regular guest on the Johnny Carson television show.

The role of Dr. Harry's Zoo in San Diego life and in the evolution of zoos worldwide is one of the brightest stories in this city's short history. San Diego is known now around the world. Its population is about ten times greater than when Dr. Harry died. And yet no San Diego institution is more revered than his Zoo. So perhaps some kernel of instruction may be lodged within these pages for those who seek to ensure this city's continuing distinction. Probably Dr. Harry would scoff at the thought; it was the animals he was thinking of, and what he did was for them.

As in the 1953 edition, I thank his widow Rachel and a host of family and friends who helped me know a distinguished San Diegan who was gone before I came. Like his widow, most of them are now gone too. They include Belle Benchley, his great friend and aide, who directed the Zoo through the years of World War II and until Charlie Schroeder's arrival; and Dr. Harry's sister Emma Tyler. Among his friends, Tom Faulconer, Waldo Malmberg, Milton Leeper, Mrs. Dudley Burlingame, and Cyrus Perkins were most helpful. Valuable source material came from the pages of the *San Diego Union*, the *San Diego Tribune*, the *San Diego Sun*, and ZOONOOZ.

Two Wegeforth sons survive: Lester Paul and Milton, who served 40 years as trustee of the Zoo his father founded and retains the title of trustee emeritus. A public school and child care centers in San Diego carry forward the Wegeforth name.

A brief epilogue for this edition has been written by Tom Scharf, historian and editor of ZOONOOZ.

Neil Morgan

La Jolla, California
October 13, 1990

PART ONE

THE ROAR BEGINS

by Neil Morgan

Future founder of the San Diego Zoo, seven-year-old Harry M. Wegeforth doffs his cap.

Backyard Zoo Keeper

On North Avenue in Baltimore there lived a lady who normally did not keep garter snakes in her home. Her first memory of Harry Wegeforth is that he convinced her she needed three of them, and that she should pay him well for them. The other thing she remembers from that same disturbing day is that he wore his necktie around his leg.

Later, as a man, Harry Wegeforth moved his necktie to his neck. But in the other trait he never changed. The San Diego Zoo was built largely with money, animals, and materials that he convinced others they should give. He also gave the Zoo most of his own money, and most of his time. The Zoo became a multi-million-dollar display of his unselfish promotional genius.

His father, Conrad Wegefarth, was a court stenographer in southwest Germany who walked more than three hundred miles through winter snow to stow away on a ship for America. Landing at Baltimore, he walked once more—this time to Pittsburgh, and a job as clerk in a dry goods store. Twelve years later, already twice a widower with six sons, Conrad Wegefarth launched his own oil refining business. In London and Paris he demonstrated coal oil lamps, forging the market for coal oil in Europe. Back in the United States, he gambled heavily in oil development, and by 1873—though a county in Texas had been named for him—he was bankrupt.

In 1867 he had married his third wife, Mary Elizabeth McArthur, a handsome girl of Scotch-Irish descent. Seven more children came to Conrad Wegefarth: five sons, each of whom went into the study of medicine, and two daughters, Emma and Ellen. Three of the sons later were to practice medicine in San Diego: Arthur, Paul, and Harry—who changed the spelling of the family name from Wegefarth to Wegeforth.

The home in Baltimore where Harry Wegeforth was born had a glistening white marble front. Even that has been displaced by a theater, at the intersection of North and Charles Avenues. The entertainment hysteria of that neighborhood in 1882, the year of his birth, was not theater—but the Barnum and Bailey circus, which pitched its tents nearby. It may not have been the circus that led the boy Harry to give his mother a china owl for her birthday when he was seven, but circus life became an early obsession of his childhood. From it grew a genuine understanding of animal life, which swelled into the obsession of his adult life—the creation of a zoo, dedicated at his insistence to "the children of San Diego."

At nine, he opened his own circus in a neighbor's back yard. The animals were toy animals. Flour bags were stitched together for the big top, and the center pole was an umbrella stick. Only once did live animals go on display—a pair of ducks—and then the show was interrupted abruptly by a Baltimore policeman who had reason to believe the ducks belonged at a nearby poultry shop.

Wegeforth was a United States Army captain during World War I. While he awaited transportation overseas, the Armistice was signed, and he then returned to San Diego.

Unlike most children who play at circuses, Harry Wegeforth went into laborious research on the habits and characteristics of his "kangaroo," his "giraffe," or his "lion." At every chance he studied live animal life, crabbing in Chesapeake Bay or snake-hunting in the woods outside Baltimore. It was not to be much different forty years later, as he drove up Pacific Coast Highway from San Diego to Los Angeles with his wife, and braked his car to a screeching stop to trap a badger at the roadside—for his Zoo.

Close observation of visiting circuses led young Harry to a conviction that he would make a splendid tightrope walker. As circus performers trained in their winter quarters nearby, he became an observant understudy to the tightrope walkers. At twelve, he persuaded the performers to give him a chance. At the end of his second winter of practice with them, he was taken into their act and began to tour. But an elder brother, Charles, brought him home and abruptly ended his circus career.

His school life had been erratic and undistinguished. Now he tried harder, resigned that he would follow his older brothers into medical study. At fifteen, he had turned so much of his absorbed interest into this field that he earned a position with the Baltimore Health Department. But again he was frustrated. Hurrying across the city in a snowstorm on an errand for the Health Department, he contracted influenza and within weeks—examining his own slides under a microscope—discovered he was suffering from acute tuberculosis.

When only sixteen, he took the medical advice of a brother and moved to Colorado—where for almost four years he rode as a cowboy, punching cattle on the Colorado plains and riding night herd on longhorns. Living on sow belly and sour-

Rachel Granger married Wegeforth on November 14, 1913. She was 20 and he was 31.

dough biscuit, he made a permanent recovery from tuberculosis. Meanwhile, by correspondence course, he completed his high school training. When he returned to Baltimore, cured, he entered the University of Maryland. With the family fortune depleted, he worked in drug stores and taught anatomy during winter months to support himself in college training; during the summer, he worked on the farm of a sister-in-law.

Graduating from Baltimore Medical College, the young physician took a position as assistant bacteriologist for the city of Baltimore, and soon afterward became first surgeon of the Baltimore Northeastern Dispensary.

But the same restless urge that had brought his father to this country led the son westward in 1908. Searching for a place in which to open a new medical practice, he stepped off a train in Jamestown, North Dakota, on a day when the temperature had dropped below zero. That was enough. The next train westward was flagged, and the young physician swung back aboard. Starting at Seattle and traveling southward, Harry Wegeforth reached San Diego, and stayed. Promptly, he passed the California State Board of Medicine examinations, borrowed $50, and opened offices at the corner of Fifth Avenue and Broadway—then known as D Street.

In the San Diego tradition, he was soon followed to the city by his sister Emma, who became his housekeeper and medical secretary; then in 1915 he was followed by his brother Paul, a distinguished brain surgeon who joined him in San Diego practice but died in 1923; and by his brother Arthur, who practiced medicine in San Diego until his death in 1939, as head of the San Diego Hospital-Clinic.

In his first months at San Diego, Harry Wegeforth was finding the pattern that would enable him later to build the San Diego Zoo. To treat ailing prisoners at county jail, he was called frequently by Sheriff Fred M. Jennings—whose daughter, Belle Benchley, many years later became executive secretary of the Zoo that Wegeforth was yet to establish.

Then there was a pretty girl named Rachel Granger. In 1892, her father, Ralph, had come to San Diego with a deep faith in the future of the city, bought a bank, and built the Granger Building at Fifth Avenue and Broadway. Wegeforth began to visit the Granger girl in her home at Third Avenue and Laurel Street. She was 20—and he 31—when they married on November 14, 1913.

Promptly after the ceremony, the doctor and his wife drove away toward the hills of San Diego County in his new Overland car. A wheel rolled off near Escondido. Near Santa Ysabel, two tires went flat. The unhappy groom persuaded an Indian to hitch four mules to the honeymoon car and drag it into nearby Mesa Grande. The couple took the bus home finally, to find their new home flooded from broken water pipes.

Wegeforth's brother, Dr. Paul Wegeforth, also served in World War I. The two men were named surgeons in 1916 for San Diego's Panama-California International Exposition.

Harry Wegeforth's most immediate concern, in that first moment, was to rescue a dozen Japanese fantail fish whose pond had been flooded by the mishap.

That was three years before San Diego had a zoo.

This Was the Roar

The Wegeforth brothers—Harry and Paul—were named surgeons in 1916 for the Panama-California International Exposition in San Diego's Balboa Park. Circumstances were closing in on Harry Wegeforth.

During the following years, his story of the founding of the San Diego Zoo in 1916 was to become one of the classic oversimplifications of the city's history. In the same way that he abhorred to see his name in print during those years, he understated the extraordinary vision that led from the roar of a lonely lion on display at the Exposition—to the creation of a zoo.

Tom Faulconer, one of his closest friends then and later a director of the Zoo, said it this way:

> No one person gave so much of his personal energy, interest, devotion and very life to the development of a public project as Doctor Harry gave to the creation of the Zoo. Certainly no benefactor was more self-effacing. As the half dozen moth-eaten monkeys, coyotes and bears left over from the Exposition developed through the years into an institution of international repute, reporters and magazine writers eagerly followed its progress. After Doctor Harry had told his story, he invariably concluded an interview this way: "Just leave my name out."

To those who tramp through the canyons and over the mesas of the San Diego Zoo today, or ride buses along its trails past hundreds of cages, grottoes and corrals, or rest beneath trees and shrubs gathered from every continent, it cannot be apparent how wildly impossible it seemed to the people of San Diego in 1916 that so small a city, in a remote corner of the nation, should aspire to a zoological garden vying in importance with those of the world's oldest and largest cities.

By 1916, through reading and travel, this San Diego physician had become an expert on animal care and display. Styles of zoo architecture intrigued him. As he rode his Arabian stallion about the still barren hills of Balboa Park, under the benevolent Southern California sun, he made his plans.

In many ways, they were revolutionary in zoo design. Moats were used in conjunction with deep canyons and precipitous mesas to make caging of even lions and bears unnecessary. Animals were brought close to the people with a minimum of cage effect.

Climate eliminated the need for general heating, and for much of the shelter normally necessary in zoos. Climate also made possible subtropical landscaping that rebuilt natural environments for many animals and also provided, for some, the leaves and fruit of their native habitats.

Always cost-conscious, Harry Wegeforth announced his intention of providing more zoo for the money than any other in the world. Men who have given their whole careers to zoo work since have agreed that he succeeded.

But conception was not all the battle. He made forays along the waterfront to "beg" fish to feed his animal family. He led excursions to outlying ranches and beseeched farmers to donate hay. In those first years of the Zoo, he himself collected second-grade fruits and vegetables from the produce markets of San Diego and brought them to the Zoo.

He inspired the strong cooperation of the San Diego press, but, when necessary, he could even outsmart newsmen. In the summer of 1917, a *San Diego Union* photographer asked that he produce a stork to stand for a picture with three newborn lion cubs. Harry Wegeforth's little zoo had no stork. But he promptly came up with a pelican, and the photographer submitted happily.

The San Diego Zoo originally consisted of rows of cages along Park Boulevard. Dr. Wegeforth (right) during the 1920s with three new tiger cubs.

Dr. Wegeforth astride his Arabian stallion while exploring Zoo property. Much of the early Zoo was empty parkland (below and below, right) that Wegeforth developed according to his ideas.

By December 1917, after little over a year of operation, the San Diego Zoo won a press association tribute as the finest collection of animals on the West Coast.

Rejected at the outbreak of World War I for military service, Harry Wegeforth reapplied to the Army Medical Board and in July 1918, was commissioned as captain and assigned to the Neuro-Surgical Institute of New York for training. He was awaiting immediate transportation overseas when the Armistice was signed. Back he came to a thriving San Diego medical practice—and his zoo.

New cages were needed before animals fell through the shaky floors of existing cages. More land was needed, too. Bluntly, he stepped before city council and asked for almost ten percent of the vast acreage of San Diego's Balboa Park. He met an almost solid front of residents and city officials who believed the Park must be kept sacrosanct for flowers, art, and music.

Patiently, he began to interest city officials, one by one, in the work of the Zoo. He gained his natural allies, the children of the city, through free admission, free lectures, and elephant rides.

And gradually, men and women who had little enthusiasm for parks or zoos, and who scoffed at his apparently fantastic plans, began to respect the persistence of this doctor who was wild for animals. Over to his side were drawn prominent architects, engineers, builders, artists, writers, and educators. As his friend Faulconer says: "Doctor Harry became the hub of a great wheel that began to roll with increasing momentum. The suite of offices which, as a busy and very successful physician, he maintained downtown, resembled the headquarters of a vast building project, as in fact it was. Contractors, material men, and designers were sandwiched in between patients, and blueprints and construction schedules covered tables, desks, and, on occasion, even his operating tables."

In his diaries, the doctor summed up these early years with a casualness that belies the aggressive battle he waged: "It took ordinary persistence, and the organization of teamwork among others. I tried never to lose heart. Whenever anybody started to knock my plans, I just kept right on boosting them. The idea of failure never entered my mind. Of course it was hard at first, but when they saw I was really making good, that I meant business and San Diego was going to have a high class zoo, they came through nobly."

Yet, astoundingly, newspaper clippings and early records of the Zoo are significant for a major omission—the name of the president and founder of the Zoo, Harry Wegeforth, almost never appeared. Credit went to men like Louis J. Gill, architect, who donated his work; to Lester Olmstead, who built much of the Zoo as contractor and often without much profit; to A. T. Mercier, later president of Southern Pacific Railways, but then a major factor in helping Harry Wegeforth reach wealthy patrons for contributions to the Zoo; and to yachtsmen like Capt. Allan Hancock and Fred Lewis, who led expeditions for new specimens to add to the Zoo.

The herculean role of Harry Wegeforth in founding the San Diego Zoo is summarized in this paragraph in an early guidebook available to Zoo visitors:

> His job was that of manager, promoter, planner, financial advisor, and much of the time in the early days he was the sole support. Practically alone, he raised all the private funds with which the magnificent Zoo was built. He visualized and planned all of its unique features. He traveled at his own expense all over the world, bringing back ideas not only from zoos, but from parks, natural scenery, and from conversations with people famous for the work they had done in their native country. He made connections which enabled the Zoological Society to obtain not only zoological exhibits, but rare shrubs and trees. It was through his interest in the relationship between diseases of wild animals and his own experience in human medicine that our Zoological Hospital was planned and built.

All this he did, during long luncheon hours and on weekends and vacations. His medical practice simultaneously grew more demanding. Instead of lunching downtown near his offices, he began to perch on a stool at the Zoo, gulping a sandwich and dictating letters—buying or selling animals—and conferring with a small staff over individual problems of animal health or of construction.

To him this did not mean pressure or hardship. "A zoo," he said, "is just about the most fascinating place in the world. And it gives you a sense of awe to be responsible for so many strange animals. It takes a little time usually to find out what they want, but that's the most fun of all."

Man Without a Turtle

Big words come readily after a big man is gone.

But Harry Wegeforth was not a man who understood or enjoyed lofty phrases. He read voraciously and with unsophisticated tastes. His favorite author was Rudyard Kipling, and his favorite story was "Kim." Yet no scholar could preen his knowledge

Dr. Wegeforth loved turtles and tortoises. He continued to trade for them at zoos around the world until the San Diego Zoo had the finest collection anywhere.

before this physician—without risk of a deft squelch.

Once a visiting magazine writer, who tended toward the pompous, was touring the Zoo with Harry Wegeforth. The doctor listened politely to the visitor's elaborate discussions of the animals—and gave no evidence of the impatience that was mounting within him. Finally the writer paused in front of a pool, and asked what was inside.

"Mirounga angustirostris," replied Wegeforth, unsmiling, and moved on as a baby elephant seal splashed its head above the water.

More big words popped up in 1936, on a happy day when the Wegeforth Bowl, the amphitheater within Zoo grounds, was decorated with a plaque at the behest of the doctor's many friends. Midway through a ceremony that seemed mildly embarrassing to the doctor, a brisk breeze tore aside the cloth that veiled the plaque and led to an abrupt dedication. These were the words:

> From earth's far distant reaches, he brought the beasts of the soil, the birds of the air and the fish of the sea, that all might learn the wonders of created life. The San Diego Zoological Gardens is the living monument to his ideals, faith and courage. Dedicated to Dr. Harry Wegeforth, founder and president of the Zoological society of San Diego, whose wide vision and untiring labor secured this zoological collection and planted this garden for the instruction and enjoyment of the people.

Harry Wegeforth scanned the words intently at the unveiling and registered polite recognition. He seemed touched but vaguely injured.

"Well," he said, turning to his friends, "it's nice. But you could have bought an animal with the money."

At another dedication ceremony—when the two elephants donated by John D. Spreckels were presented to the children of San Diego in 1923, before a large crowd—Harry Wegeforth refused even to go near the speaker's platform. He turned the introduction of Spreckels over to Representative George Burnham and Senator Samuel Shortridge. Wegeforth's role, as usual, was backstage. This time it was mischievous. He sent a note to the podium that was promptly read to the audience of hundreds—that the Senator and Spreckels would ride the elephants at the conclusion of the ceremony.

With a knowing glower in the direction of Wegeforth, both men rose promptly to decline that honor. Wegeforth's delighted guffaw could be heard around the Zoo.

Mixed with the intense concentration, the tinge of genius, and the delight that this man sensed in challenge, could be found the paradoxical frustrations of a Walter Mitty. His letters are peppered with protests to manufacturers and salesmen over the things he bought that never worked.

Once, he bought a razor strop dressing from a San Diego hardware shop and was so irritated when it failed to soften his strop that he wrote the manufacturer. Back came

Dedication of plaque for Dr. Harry Wegeforth at Wegeforth Bowl in 1936.

another jar of the dressing and a regretful note that the hardware supply was obviously old and hardened beyond value. The president of the San Diego Zoo took time to write once again to the manufacturer, reporting that the second jar fulfilled its purpose admirably.

He loved big cars. In 1923, he went into debt to buy an eight-cylinder Packard equipped with every accessory in the manufacturer's catalog. Then he paid to repaint the new car fire-engine red. Within a year he was dissatisfied and traded cars again.

While he was in the Orient, his California physician's license was revoked because he was not home to pay a $2 renewal fee. Returning, he was faced with a $10 penalty fee. He carried his protest to the California Medical Association and threatened to wage a campaign to repeal the fee in the State Legislature. But this time he got nowhere. Music was one of his dearest retreats. He pored over catalogs of new phonographs and record changers and wrote to manufacturers to discuss coming models. But they seldom worked well enough to meet his severe standards.

Perhaps the strangest petty frustration of his entire life was a home in Duncan, Oklahoma, which he accepted in lieu of a large medical bill in 1921. It was almost fifteen years before he could let loose of that home, and it had become the steadiest loser of any of his investments. In his correspondence is a two-inch-thick file of letters from agents, tax collectors, bankers, and mortgage holders—telegrams threatening seizure and seeking authorization for repairs, all on a home that rented through most of the depression for $5 a month. Finally, a harried real estate agent in Duncan, whom Wegeforth had retained to handle the property, decided that he would take a picture of the home and mail it to Wegeforth. That did it. It was one of the most desolate shacks of a desolate town, and Wegeforth agreed promptly on a sale that brought $300—less than one-sixth the figure of the medical bill he had settled fifteen years before.

He flitted from one hobby to another. First he built radios. Later he took up shooting. Then came cameras, and finally he had hit on a hobby that integrated with his Zoo. His sons Milton and Lester treasure a vast collection of color slides that recorded not only his "family" at the Zoo but also his tours around the world in the final years of his life.

He was a 32nd-degree Mason and at some time a member of every major social and country club in San Diego. He enjoyed football and baseball but participated actively only in horseback riding. He never swam and urged his family against it—in the terrible memory of the drowning of his brother Charles during his boyhood in Baltimore.

If among all the animals he loved there were favorites, these were the turtles. From every trip he returned with turtles. Around his desk at the Zoo he gathered turtles in plaster, in silver, and in oil. His favorite photograph was of his son, Lester, astride a giant tortoise.

And when a famed New York zoo official visited the San Diego Zoo, Harry Wegeforth adopted his most plaintive manner and inquired:

"Why is it nobody ever gives me any turtles? I'm always wanting some turtles. Can't you send me some turtles?"

The New Yorker politely walked out toward the turtle exhibits, pencil and notebook in hand, to jot down what species were already on exhibit at the Zoo as a guide toward choosing turtles for a shipment to San Diego.

He was back in five minutes and stood in front of Wegeforth, helpless with laughter.

"I have just visited your turtle basins," he told the doctor. "All forty-eight of them you damn rascal! This is the biggest collection of turtles in the world!"

Animal Lobbyist

Politicians grew to respect Harry Wegeforth. Even the honest ones. He had an early brush with politics as president of the San Diego Board of Health—an abrupt and violent assignment—and he had little regard for the manipulations of most city hall inhabitants. Towards them he could be gentle and smiling—if they were nurturing his

Zoo. But if they failed to do his bidding, he lashed out at them with an indiscriminate violence that became the delight of the San Diego citizenry.

He appeared to have the city administration baffled from the start. He churned up such a roar of civic protests against the tragic condition of the Exposition animals in 1916 that the city council was helpless against his demand for city land for a zoo.

Over a decade later, he submitted to city council a map and charter amendment that would dedicate Zoo grounds for all time and ban bisecting city streets or roads. A week after approving his map, councilmen found, in a flash of dismay, that the map showed eight additional acres adjoining the Zoo grounds that they had turned over to this persistent physician and his Zoological Society. Wegeforth wanted the acreage because it surrounded the new research and hospital building at the Zoo.

City Attorney Shelley Higgins rose before the councilmen and newspaper reporters and intoned: "It is unfortunate if the council did not realize the exact limits described in the amendment and relief map produced by Dr. Wegeforth, because they have been available for over a week."

Wegeforth bowed discreetly, and disappeared from council chambers for a few weeks. The land was the Zoo's.

One of Dr. Wegeforth's favorite photographs was this one, which includes his son Lester, astride a giant tortoise, at the Zoo.

About that time, the Nolen Plan was advanced for the development of San Diego. Harry Wegeforth studied it and found it good—except for roads that it proposed, bisecting the north and south ends of his rambling Zoo. Now Wegeforth went forth to do battle with the Park Commission, on which sat George Marston and W. Templeton Johnson, two of the city's great leaders. Wegeforth brushed them aside.

"This Nolen Plan," roared the doctor, "is a beautifully colored thing and looks fine as a map. But the citizens of this community have spent $330,000 on their zoo while the city has provided only $60,000. More then 300,000 people visit the zoo annually. These proposed roads would destroy every pond and den in the canyon. You gentlemen know nothing of animals. You have already given us these grounds."

George Marston jumped to his feet that day at city hall.

"If the roads would interfere with the seals," said he, "the doctor could remove them. I've given 20 years of my life to the Park, too."

Wegeforth struck back.

"The promises of the Park Board are not worth a pinch of snuff. They have backed down on them time and time before."

This was too much for the respected Marston to take. Usually one of the most reserved of public figures, he shouted this time:

"That's wrong! I didn't used to be a scrapper, but I learned how to be one from Dr. Wegeforth!"

No roads bisected the Zoo, then or now.

A few months later, the city calmly granted to the Zoo the $36,000 for operating costs that the Zoo president, Harry Wegeforth, told them would be necessary for 1928. This was a calm session, indeed. Newspapers reported that "Dr. Wegeforth appeared briefly in support of the request, and went away happy."

One of the most fabulous of Wegeforth's wrestling matches with the Park Commission concerned a 23-foot python named Diablo, which would not eat unless held by a score of men and had food forced down its throat. This grisly spectacle, occurring every several months, became one of the most popular events of Zoo history. When almost 10,000 persons appeared to witness a feeding in 1924, Wegeforth decided that he had happened on an excellent lever for Zoo public relations, and decided to move the show for the next feeding to the Park Stadium. Admission was to be charged for adults—but not, in the Zoo tradition, for children. Yet the Park Commission warned Wegeforth that it must receive the usual two-cent "take" on each person admitted to the Stadium for any event.

The physician was astonished. He felt this to be a nonprofit occasion for a nonprofit organization—the Zoo—and insisted that the Park Commission should waive its royalty on the children's admissions.

The 23-foot python named Diablo would not eat unless held by a number of men and force-fed,

The Commission, however, was adamant.

Wegeforth went forthwith to the newspapers: "It's going to be hard on the children," he stated slyly, and this was front-page news:

> Lots of them won't have a dime and the park men will chase them. We asked for the Stadium so that people would not be crowded half to death and so they could sit down in comfort and watch the python being fed. If the people of San Diego want a Zoo in the park, and 8000 or 10,000 people visit and enjoy the Zoo every week, it's about time they told the Park Commission about it, because yesterday's high-handed action is typical of what the Zoo authorities have enjoyed from the Park Commission. If the people don't want a Zoo, it can be eliminated in 60 days, or we can turn it over to the Park Commission and let it die a natural death.

The blister had been raised, and the heat was on.

On the eve of the feeding of Diablo in the Stadium, Park Commissioner Hugo Klauber announced that a special meeting of the Park Commission had been held and children under 12 would be admitted free. Wegeforth pushed his luck. He ordered his men to be on hand at the gates to insure that a "liberal interpretation" of the age limit as 12 be given.

Queenie the elephant gives rides, c. 1920s.

His longest campaign at city hall—one that endured for more than fifteen years from the start of the Zoo—was to win autonomous operation for the Zoo. It has been built on city land and leaned on city and county for annual grants to foster its growth. But Wegeforth had seen the tragedy of zoos in cities where their control was mingled with political intrigue, and where men having no sympathy with zoo problems were allowed to direct their operation. He had determined that the Zoo that he had nurtured so carefully—and into which he had invested so much of his own time and money without hope of return other than the fulfillment of a dream—should not risk destruction in this way.

As early as 1924, Wegeforth went before city council and said that he must know "where the Zoo stood, instead of having to go blindly before Council each year for assistance." At this time he asked that a municipal commission be created to direct the Zoo, bypassing the Park Commission with which he feuded so frequently. In the following year, such a proposal was put on the city ballot—and, because of personal animosities which had developed, became a boiling issue. The proposal was that the Zoological Society—of which Wegeforth was president—should have complete control over operation of the Zoo, free from city interference.

"Under the present plan," Wegeforth insisted in a debate before the Woman's Club, "we must submit plans of our landscape architect to a board, the members of which admittedly know nothing of landscape architecture."

This paradox impressed the ladies, and they applauded.

The Zoological Society won—and holds today—control over operation of the Zoo, although grounds and equipment are in technical possession of the City of San Diego. But it was another decade before Wegeforth was able to triumph on an alternate goal—a two-cent per $100 valuation city tax, written into charter law, to go automatically and without diversion into support of the Zoo.

During this long fight, Wegeforth gave vent to one of his rare displays of fatigue where Zoo work was concerned.

"I've put thousands of dollars into the Zoo," he told city council. "I've been able to get others to give liberally. I've worked for the interests of the Zoo for 11 years. But unless the city will grant a stipulated fund which may not be cut off at the will of the Park Commission, I am through with the Zoo."

Councilmen saw their duty, and did it: they promptly passed a resolution praising Wegeforth for his work and put the tax measure on the ballot. It was to be there four times—winning at the polls each time but being thrown out three times on technical grounds—before its final success. When the last fight for the tax was waged in 1934, much of the political load was carried by Belle Benchley, already executive secretary of

Dr. Wegeforth strikes a winsome pose with a lion cub. Young animals were always a favorite with the public.

the Zoo, Fred Annable of the board, and others. Wegeforth was in extreme pain during most of the final campaign as a result of the heart attack that had forced curtailment of his medical practice. The final battle was full of drama. Four councilmen who had disregarded the prescribed petitions, signed by 12,000 citizens, and voted not to put the Zoo tax on the civic ballot, were accused by the grand jury of misconduct.

Zoo business on two occasions forced Harry Wegeforth into court.

Frank Buck, the famed "Bring 'em Back Alive" explorer, was retained in 1923 as director of the Zoo, on a three-year contract. But Wegeforth and the board terminated his services after several sharp disagreements. Buck sued for $12,500 in salary that he would have received and $10,000 in damages. A sensational trial rolled on for almost a week. Finally Curtis Hillyer, counsel for the Zoo, rose to begin his closing arguments. Superior Judge Charles N. Andrews interrupted him to rule that no further arguments would be necessary, since evidence showed clearly that Buck had disobeyed orders of the Zoological Society and his discharge had been warranted.

Another court appearance had its ludicrous tinge.

■ ANIMAL LOBBYIST 39

As climax to a long negotiation over ownership of a building near the Zoo, Patrick F. O'Rourke in 1932 swore out a complaint that Wegeforth had "threatened to knock my block off." Wegeforth appeared for a scheduled jury trial, and a crowd pushed into court chambers. Reporters and photographers waited eagerly—but O'Rourke did not appear.

A subpoena was handed down promptly from the bench, and court attaches fanned out over the city to hunt down the plaintiff. They found him just a block away, at ease in the Cuyamaca Club. Hailed into court, he told the judge he didn't care any longer to testify against his friend Harry Wegeforth. The charge was dropped.

And Harry Wegeforth rushed out of court and back to his Zoo.

Animal Trader Frank Buck was retained in 1923 as director of the Zoo. Along with Zoological Society board members, Dr. Wegeforth would later terminate the arrangement.

Photo from All in a Lifetime, by Frank Buck.

One of the Zoo's early tigers — perhaps a patient of Dr. Wegeforth's?

Doctor to a Tiger

Harry Wegeforth, physician and surgeon, watched anxiously as a new tiger at the San Diego Zoo writhed in pain, suddenly sinister and treacherous. Veterinarians had decided there was intestinal trouble. But handlers found the animal too dangerous to try to rope and tie for treatment.

"I wonder," mused Wegeforth, pausing to chuckle with his teeth clenched tight, "if I can't toss some tablets into his mouth."

The handlers stared at him as at a child.

"Sure," quipped one. "Just tell him to open wide."

Wegeforth disappeared, and returned in ten minutes with a bottle of calomel tablets. Before keepers could interfere he had entered the cage and approached the tiger. The animal crouched, ready to spring.

Just then his gigantic jaws opened, his teeth flashed wickedly, and the man standing in front of him casually tossed a handful of tablets into the pink, cavernous mouth.

The spring of the animal was broken. Astonished, he slipped off balance and drew back, gulping the strange, tiny tablets in his mouth.

Waving away the keepers, Wegeforth waited once more for the tiger to start his spring and part his jaws. Once more he landed a handful of tablets squarely in the animal's mouth.

This time the tiger retired and moved toward his water supply for natural aid in swallowing the strange objects tossed into his mouth.

But two nights before, Harry Wegeforth had been called on to talk at a civic function. He rose, his own mouth dry, his hands trembling, and excused himself without explanation.

Though seldom displaying such foolhardy daring—unless feeling there was no other way to save an animal—Harry Wegeforth brought his medical knowledge into play frequently to aid his "family" at the San Diego Zoo. As a routine, he cared for the medical needs of his Zoo staff, almost always without charge. But the ailments of the animals were usually far more challenging to him.

Because of his keen knowledge of animal behavior, he was able to transpose his medical background with uncanny success to the treatment of animals. He served as consultant to Zoo veterinarians. Often a veterinarian would telephone him during the night when an animal became seriously ill. The doctor would go to the side of the animal just as he would to a human patient—and often was able to suggest a method of treatment that led to recovery. Mrs. Dudley Burlingame, who for many years was employed in the Zoo hospital, believes that much of his success stemmed from his respect for each animal as an individual—and his ability to sense the significance of each animal's symptoms.

He studied animal tuberculosis and cancer at the Zoo laboratories and did notable research in hoof and mouth disease. Even before the Zoo was established, he had turned over to the Department of Agriculture in Washington a remedy for black-head in turkeys, a disease which at that time had caused a virtual abandonment of turkey growing in sections of the nation.

He bought cod liver oil in fifty-gallon drums for his lions and had other zoos guessing for years on how he achieved such glossy black manes on the lions he bred in San Diego. He was a strong disciple of force-feeding captured animals who refused food. From the start, the San Diego Zoo set new records in low casualties of animals due to disease.

Actually, the capability of Harry Wegeforth as a physician and surgeon often was submerged in the glitter of his work with the Zoo. But he made a startling rise in practice from the moment, as a restless youth, he opened offices in San Diego. He developed a keen interest in bone surgery and traveled to medical centers in Baltimore and New York on several occasions for special studies in surgery techniques. Invited on one such occasion to assist at a delicate brain operation just being developed, he was unexpectedly given the entire assignment before a gallery of medical students. One witness to his performance reports that his dexterity was so superb that the gallery rose spontaneously at the conclusion of the operation in tribute to the San Diego man.

One of his most faithful aides at the Zoo, Mrs. Dudley Burlingame, traces her acquaintance with Harry Wegeforth to the day that she rushed into his offices with her six-year-old son, whose leg had been crushed under a tractor several days before in Mexico. Because the leg was distended and gangrenous, the doctor ruled that amputation would be necessary to save the child's life. But she pleaded with him so hysterically against the cut that he spent most of the night draining the leg in a desperate effort to save it. The child did not walk again for eleven months—but by then the leg was unimpaired and normal.

The medical career of Harry Wegeforth was, however, often a turbulent one—largely because of the restless drive that characterized all of his actions. Only four years after his arrival in San Diego, he found himself appointed as president of the City Board of Health.

There, he saw a job to do—and impetuously swung into it full blast, launching drives for purification of milk and foodstuffs, bacteria tests among all food suppliers, and publication of the names of substandard suppliers. Here he collided with politics for the first time. Because he felt the mayor and city council were not backing his attempted reforms, he loosed one of his famed blasts against them in the newspapers. Stung, Mayor James E. Wadham abruptly fired Wegeforth.

For the first time, Wegeforth found himself a civic hero. He was lauded in an editorial in the *San Diego Sun:*

> The Sun bears no brief for Doctor Wegeforth, who, by the way, seems quite able to take care of himself in almost any emergency, but common decency compels some public recognition of the services which Dr. Wegeforth has rendered San Diego while he has been at the head of the City Board of Health. He has worked hard and long and courageously against that old-fossilized regime which has done little or nothing to stop unclean meat, poor milk and carelessly kept foodstuffs, along with a suspicion of petty graft among subordinates in the city service . . . If what Dr. Wegeforth has been doing is 'incompetence,' as charged, then what the city seems to need is some more of the same kind of incompetence . . . .

As his practice broadened, his prowess as a diagnostician became widely known. A longtime superintendent of nurses in a leading San Diego hospital recalled recently how she had felt: "I'd rather have Doctor Harry make a snap judgment and operate on me than to have five opinions and all the tests, because he had a big heart and understanding of the suffering and symptoms of sick people."

Because of his nature, he dedicated an unusual amount of time to work among charity patients and dreamed of establishing a clinic that would cater especially to low-income patients. Throughout the twenties he spent several weeks each year observing hospital operation and surgical techniques in major cities. By 1928, on the eve of the depression, he was ready to open what he hoped would fulfill his medical dream—the San Diego Hospital-Clinic. Financed with the aid of his wife, the hospital was located at Seventh Avenue and G Street, even closer then than now to the actual

The goat "mountain" is an early Zoo exhibit that is attributed to Dr. Wegeforth.

hub of downtown San Diego. It was a three-story building with 47 beds, and the basement was especially equipped for physiotherapy, in conjunction with his specialty of bone surgery.

But this creative dream was not destined to have the success of the Zoo. It was marred by depression, unfortunate location, and a previous disagreement with the Medical Society (from which he emerged in the right) stemming from his initiative in industrial accident and hospital plans while surgeon for the San Diego, Arizona and Eastern Railway. The final blow came in December, 1931, when he rose from a serious case of influenza to operate on the crushed elbow of a small girl. At the end of the operation he collapsed from a coronary thrombosis and angina. He was never able to resume his medical practice. Heart specialists who saw him frequently in the remaining decade of his life believe that only his own medical skill and diagnostic acumen kept him alive through the years he believed necessary to complete the building of the San Diego Zoo.

Only one wry fragment of humor is remembered by most San Diego citizens today when Harry Wegeforth's ill-fated hospital is recalled. It is of a protest that was filed with city council, asking that his hospital be designated a public nuisance—because the squalling of newborn babies in the maternity ward was disturbing residents of an adjoining rooming house. Councilmen, who were as loathe by then to arouse Wegeforth as they were to attack the stork, quietly filed the protest.

A trail and small bridge show the openness of Zoo grounds during the 1920s. The photograph opposite is dated 1922 and depicts a small dam planned as part of a future seal enclosure.

Though Wegeforth largely stepped out of medical practice after his heart attack, the hospital continued in operation for several years and finally was sold as a rooming house, which it remains today.

The collapse of the hospital venture, bringing a sour anticlimax to a medical practice that had been memorable, left a deep scar in the doctor's heart. One of the bluntest recorded documents of his feelings—and interesting evidence of the good humor that managed to pervade most of his actions, despite disappointment—can be found in a letter that he wrote in 1937 to his friend Nat Rogan, then of the Internal Revenue Department in Los Angeles:

Dear Nat,

In 1935 I was running a hospital and was supposed to be making some money, but I didn't. I don't know how it was, for I never received any cash out of it and lost everything I had. Now, the government says I am to pay them $275. The notice came to the house and I mislaid it or something happened to it. I don't want to go to jail, and I won't have any money until next month. Will you please let me know when the deadline is on this payment. Best regards and hoping that you had a very successful year with your incomes.

Your friend,

Harry Wegeforth, M.D.
President, San Diego Zoo

Promoter and Surgeon

"Watch out for this Wegeforth," John D. Spreckels, a founding father of San Diego, once said. "If you're a patient, you get your tonsils or your appendix out. But if you're working on the Zoo, you get cut off at the pockets."

Spreckels knew. The ruse by which Wegeforth persuaded him to buy the Zoo's first elephants—powdering them white—is the classic of all Zoo stories and one which Wegeforth himself related in the manuscript that appears in this volume.

This quiet, unassuming physician was capable of becoming—for the sake of the Zoo—a zealous Robin Hood whose finesse at gathering money from the wealthy may never have been surpassed, even in Sherwood Forest. It is not unreasonable to estimate that more than a million dollars—in outright cash, contribution of animals, labor or materials—went into the building of the Zoo almost entirely because of the saucy persuasiveness of Harry Wegeforth.

Within his own personality was clear evidence of a frugal, scheming mind where money was concerned—and it is perhaps the recognition of this that appealed so often to the wealthy. They knew that their contributions to Harry Wegeforth's Zoo would be craftily multiplied by his own shrewdness. It was also obvious to the hundreds of Zoo donors that Harry Wegeforth was giving everything he had to the Zoo—and thus his ardent solicitations were freed of any stigma of selfish gain.

Still evident in construction of the Zoo today is his use of near-junk material—old boiler tubing, discarded rails, elevator cables, cement testing blocks from city laboratories, old brick and pipe. With some of this material he displayed such ingenious adaptation for Zoo use that the city crossed such material off its junk lists for the first time, so that Wegeforth unwittingly cut off a source of beggared supply for the Zoo.

The first of many gifts from Ellen Browning Scripps, patron of so many San Diego institutions, was one that appealed to her, as to Harry Wegeforth, as a sound investment:

outside fencing around the 210 acres of the Zoo, making possible for the first time, in 1922, collection of admission from adults—on which the present economy of the Zoo is largely based. Before her death, she had given the Zoo almost a quarter of a million dollars.

Wegeforth, however, had a grandiose plan.

Months before Miss Scripps' adoption of this massive fencing project, he had drawn up a candid petition to all the people of San Diego. The Zoo, he said—as he was to say many times again—had reached a crossroads of life or death. He itemized needed grottoes, cages, water and sewage systems, hospital and laboratory, abattoir and cold storage facilities—totaling in cost $106,571.

"If it is possible that the sum of money we need can be given us," he wrote, "these structures can be completed in the next six months. Then with these, we shall be well equipped to receive the many contributions from the general public."

Actually, many of these structures already were underway. Wegeforth knew how difficult it was to "sell" to a donor a project that was only on paper. Often he persuaded contractors—and even bankers—to carry a project solely on his promise that, from

Ellen Browning Scripps, a patron of many San Diego institutions, presented a number of monetary gifts to the San Diego Zoo. The first of these made it possible to fence the Zoo grounds for the first time.

somewhere, he would produce the funds to pay.

Then, in this same document, he began to dot his appeal with sage quotations: "For he that hath, to him shall be given."

Then, back to his pitch: "I believe that within ten years, the San Diego Zoo will be known as one of the best in the world, and one of the most important educational institutions in our city."

"Where there is no vision, the people perish!"

His blunt, proverb-laden appeal functioned perfectly. Within a year, he was on to new expansion projects. Already he had assured that the midtwenties would be recorded as the period during which the San Diego Zoo left behind forever any serious threat of failure.

In 1925 came a civic investigation into housing and sanitation conditions at the Zoo. Suddenly, in the midst of the turmoil, appeared the fine hand of Harry Wegeforth— insisting at city hall and before clubs that increased city and county support was desperately needed to insure the health and safety of Zoo animals. Friends shook their heads

Construction of Monkey Quadrangle in the early 1920s.

Dedication at Monkey Quadrangle—Dr. Wegeforth is crouching in the front row, fifth from the right. Funds for the enclosure were a gift from the San Diego Hotel Association.

quietly and suspected the worst—that Harry Wegeforth had "planted" a civic investigation of his own Zoo, just to spotlight the need for more money and more Zoo. Next year, the County of San Diego put an assessment for the Zoo on the annual budget.

Even entire railroads were subject to the spell of Harry Wegeforth and his Zoo. In 1924, Wegeforth bought many birds and wild animals during a trip to the East. Anxious to rush them to the Zoo at top speed, he persuaded the Southern Pacific Railroad, through his friend A. T. Mercier, to add a car for them to the ace Golden State Limited—a procedure then quite as startling as if today a passenger jet had been commandeered.

At zoo conventions, where Wegeforth was widely known and loved, the physician built a reputation for animal trading so shrewd that he earned a nickname still remembered by zoo people all over the world: "Trader" Wegeforth.

One of his wife's favorite stories of his prowess as a zoo trader is that of a San Diego businessman who lunched with Wegeforth at the Cuyamaca Club. He talked of a monkey that his wife had given to the Zoo. There were many monkeys and many gifts, and of this one Wegeforth had no knowledge. But his eyes gleamed with opportunity

The Harvester Building—left standing from Balboa Park's 1915-1916 exposition—served as an early entrance for the Zoo.

when the businessman inquired where the monkey was being displayed.

"That's the trouble," Harry Wegeforth shot back.

"What?" asked his friend.

"That monkey is a mighty spunky animal. I've felt that for his own protection, and the other monkeys' safety, he should have a special cage before we put him on display."

Wegeforth's friend raised his eyebrows. "Really that tough a little scamp, is he?"

Wegeforth nodded gravely.

"Wonder how much it would cost to make up the right kind of cage for him, Harry?"

Wegeforth brushed a hand across his forehead. "About a hundred and fifty. Only trouble, we don't have that kind of money right now."

From lunch at the Cuyamaca Club Harry Wegeforth walked back to the Zoo and visited the little monkey—which had provided such an excellent excuse for the $150 check he carried in his pocket for the Zoo.

Not all the donations, of course, were large ones. The Zoo was built also on the voluntary contributions of hundreds of animals, snakes, and birds by friends and strangers, too. And among the simple gifts was that of an 11-year-old schoolboy named Hugh

Some of the Zoo's first animals were cast-off pets from U.S. Navy ships. "Lady" bear came to the Zoo in 1922.

Lattimer, who noticed one day in 1924 that mud was being tracked into the reptile house—and asked if he might present a foot scraper to the Zoo. He went to work on his project in a school workshop with such determination that the finished job, on a concrete base, weighed nearly fifty pounds. Having no other transportation, he spent one warm Saturday afternoon lugging it for a mile to the Zoo. When he arrived, hot and tired, Harry Wegeforth heard his story—and impetuously called the board of directors to the Zoo to shake the lad's hand.

Once, while Wegeforth's back was turned, the entire Zoo nearly got away. In 1932, with Wegeforth on a seal hunt into Mexican waters, James Hervey Johnson, then county assessor, concluded that the Zoo owed the County $6,358 in back taxes. City council protested that the Zoo never had been taxed and should not now be taxed. But Johnson set his deadline and announced that on one August afternoon he would sell the Zoo and all its animals at auction to highest bidders.

More than 200 people appeared at the appointed hour—but among them were numerous city police officers, including the beloved Mike Shea, famed for his readiness to do battle. Shea gave orders that Johnson could auction all day, but nobody would leave the Zoo with anything they'd bought. The people of San Diego knew Shea well. Though Johnson ranted, not one bid was made. Finally the assessor declared the Zoo to be the property of the State of California, through tax default, and the crowd went home.

In understandable alarm, a Sacramento spokesman announced for the State of California that the San Diego Zoo did not either belong to the State, despite Johnson's action.

Then Wegeforth returned and took command. With his uncanny sense of timing, he announced that the Zoo would have to sell half of its animals to support the rest. At that, city hall felt sudden hot breath from Zoo-loving taxpayers and challenged Harry Wegeforth to find some other way out. "You've put the city on the spot," cried Acting Mayor Joseph Russo.

That was the moment he always was awaiting.

"Then," said Wegeforth, sitting back, "let's get that tax levy for the Zoo on the ballot this fall."

But among all the thousands whose generosity helped to build the Zoo, there was none with more respect for Harry Wegeforth than the proprietor of a feed store where Wegeforth ran up a $500 bill one year for the Zoo—and couldn't find the money to pay it. After considerable prodding, Wegeforth visited the proprietor and prepared to make excuses.

He walked out of that store, twenty minutes later, carrying a bill stamped "Paid in Full"—and a credit for $2,000 more in feed for his "family" at the Zoo. Behind him he left a dazed merchant who read of Harry Wegeforth's funeral a few years later—and then asked Joe Galvin, the faithful Piute Indian gardener and foreman for the Wegeforth family:

"Joe, do you guess that man will talk the angels out of their wings?"

Ice Cream and Elephants

If you had asked a San Diego schoolchild during the twenties or thirties for the name of the most important man in San Diego, you would have heard—more often than any other—the name of the man who brought the elephants and lions and tigers and gorillas to San Diego.

Harry Wegeforth loved children. And he respected them as his staunchest allies in the building of the San Diego Zoo.

"Building the Zoo was really quite easy," he wrote once, "after we found how much the children of San Diego were interested in the new and strange animals we brought

Elephant rides made Dr. Wegeforth and the Zoo a great favorite of young San Diegans.

from foreign countries. The original idea called for a small group of animals to provide an interesting place to draw people out of doors on holidays, a sort of social health insurance. But so many children began to flock in that we were impressed with the possibility of a zoological garden on a large scale."

It was Wegeforth's idea to give the children of San Diego free rides every weekend on "their" elephants at the Zoo.

A newspaper reporter asked him in 1923 if he had named the two new elephants at the Zoo.

"Why, no!" he said with twinkling eyes. "They belong to the children of the city. John Spreckels paid for them, and the fine compound in which they live, and presented them officially to the children. Let the children select the names for their pets!"

Thus came a citywide balloting—bringing in thousands of suggestions—and the names of Happy and Joy received the most votes. Harry Wegeforth promptly threw an ice cream party to christen the elephants, and scores of little guests went riding on Happy and Joy.

With these children came, for the first time, thousands of parents. Many of them became staunch allies of the budding Zoo.

By 1925, when Wegeforth was battling the Park Commission for autonomous Zoo control of the grounds, he was so certain of the enthusiasm of the children that he let them take over his political drive. Printed in the newspapers each day was a sample ballot:

EVERY CHILD'S CHANCE TO VOTE

I want my Zoo kept out of politics and would vote for Proposition No. 6 if I could vote on April 7._____

I don't care what becomes of the elephants and the ponies and the other animals and would vote against Proposition No. 6._____

Name_____

Address_____ Age_____

CLIP THIS BALLOT, MARK IT, AND BRING IT WITH YOU TO THE ZOO SATURDAY, WHERE YOU CAN CAST IT IN THE BALLOT BOXES THAT WILL BE PLACED THERE. TELL YOUR FRIENDS AND LET THEM COME AND VOTE TOO. ALL CHILDREN WHO VOTE, WHETHER THEY VOTE YES OR NO, WILL BE GIVEN ICE CREAM AND CAKE FREE, AND MAY ATTEND THE MOVIE SHOW FREE.

It seems doubtful that political annals could reveal a more insidious or assured campaign. The screams of the opposition were piercing and shrill but hollow. A prominent

One of the San Diego Zoo's first celebrity visitors was child star Jackie Coogan, who arrived on March 10, 1926, and posed with a koala.

matron charged Wegeforth with "bribing" the children of the city—in a balloting that obviously had no direct significance on the outcome of the election, but was actually a devastating coup.

Harry Wegeforth saw fit to answer her charge in the press.

"It is all right to bribe children," he answered blandly, "if the end in view is worthwhile."

Thus the cause was won.

The Zoo is dedicated—by plaque and official record—to the children of San Diego. And in legal circles there are some who believe that, even here, Harry Wegeforth was looking far ahead with business sagacity. In matters of taxation and control, ownership by "the children of San Diego" creates an obvious perpetuity. So long as there are children in San Diego, the status of the Zoo seems, to some, to be legally unshakable.

Hundreds of adult San Diegans today still treasure little thank-you cards, printed with gold seals and signed by Harry Wegeforth—proving that they brought some living animal, or snake, or bird to give to the Zoo.

As his love of children was enhanced by that for his own sons, Harry Wegeforth seemed to give deeper significance to the tie between his Zoo and the children who loved it.

Several months before his death, he wrote to Gordon Gray, an attorney who faithfully represented the Zoological Society. There was about his letter a tone of valedictory: "It isn't the Zoo that we are interested in, as much as it is the education and pleasure the children receive from this institution . . . Please accept my sincere thanks for your services, and I know I speak for thousands of children in San Diego who receive happiness and knowledge from the Zoo."

Today, the smallest children squeal with delight to find—wandering freely about the Zoo and at child's eye level—brilliantly plumed peacocks and guinea hens. They are there in numbers, not because they are rare or unusual but because they appeal to the smallest Zoo lover, for whom other zoo creatures are in a faraway, adult world.

They are one of the gifts that Harry Wegeforth planned for the children he loved so much.

Tinamou Tizzy

A shipment of South American birds arrived at the San Diego Zoo one day with three mysterious passengers. They were birds much like partridges, somber and dignified. The bird keeper thumbed through several volumes of ornithology without any success in identifying the birds by name. A council of San Diego naturalists viewed the birds but arrived at no satisfactory conclusion.

Weeks later, Harry Wegeforth returned from a trip to the East and strolled past the cages in which the birds were anonymously housed.

He called for the keeper. "Why don't you get a label on the cage for these tinamous?" he asked sternly.

To such an extent was Harry Wegeforth the leader of the Zoo throughout his lifetime. His growing staff admired him as a man who enforced rigid discipline, but tempered it with the warmth of a man who knows no rank or caste among those associated in a single cause.

"He was one of the most lovable, ornery gentlemen I have ever known," one of his co-workers once said. "He demanded sincerity, loyalty, and was suspicious of the motive of personal ambition in those who worked with him, because this was so absent in his own personality. Concerning the Zoo, he felt that things should be done his own way, but he bent his thinking whenever friendship seemed strained. And the success of the Zoo proves he was almost always right."

Such intensity of purpose brought steady development not only of his Zoo—but of Harry Wegeforth himself. For the first decade of the Zoo, he refused stubbornly to make speeches or public appearances. Suddenly, at a St. Louis convention in 1924, he found himself making a speech and enjoying it. From then on he was a steady occupant of the Zoo soapbox at luncheon and dinner affairs.

Then came a carefully planned series of projects through the years that brought the

The interior of the Scripps Flight Cage in 1923—the year of its dedication. The enclosure was designed for shore and wading birds.

Zoo close to its present physical aspect. One of his pet ideas was the construction of a flying cage for birds. Completed in 1923 as the gift of Ellen Browning Scripps, it gained wide publicity as the largest structure of its kind in the world. But even this was surpassed in 1936 by the newer, larger flight cage.

Wegeforth was astonished to find, as his zoo research continued, how little effective liaison there was between the zoos of the United States. So in 1924, in cooperation with zoological society officials from St. Louis, Missouri, and Nashville, Tennessee, he led a meeting at Hotel del Coronado in Coronado, California, at which the National Association of Zoological Executives was formed. He was named president in honor of his conception of the plan. The organization became a valuable clearing house for ideas on zoo work, interchange of specimens, and as a source of encouragement for smaller zoos.

On April 16, 1924, the National Association of Zoological Executives was formed in San Diego with Dr. Wegeforth (middle, standing) as its first president. Below, the Zoo hospital and laboratory, opened in 1926, built from funds donated by Ellen Browning Scripps.

In one year alone, 1926, Wegeforth directed the planting of 5,000 trees on the Zoo grounds—including many rare species from all over the world. In the same year, feeling it vital for the Zoo to have a regular periodical—not of scientific interest but newsy and chatty—he ushered in the publication of ZOONOOZ, its title "borrowed" from a weekly column in the *San Diego Sun* by W. B. France. His proudest addition of all in Zoo history also came in 1926: the $50,000 hospital and laboratory, another gift of Ellen Scripps, which became the talk of zoo men everywhere and a center for significant research for many years.

Belle Benchley joined his staff in 1926 as executive secretary, and she began to take from his shoulders much of the detail that the growing Zoo required to function.

"Trader" Wegeforth scooped the zoo world in 1931 by negotiating successfully with the Martin Johnsons for Mbongo and Ngagi, who grew into the two largest gorillas in captivity at that time. The San Diego Zoo became for many months one of the "hottest" news spots in the nation.

Then, bracing after the depression, the Zoo made hundreds of thousands of new friends during the 1935-36 California Pacific International Exposition in Balboa Park—as a feature within the Exposition gates. Through his powerful political contacts, Harry Wegeforth brought in for the Zoo a large share of Works Progress Administration aid in the latter years of the thirties—paving roads, establishing drainage, building cages, remodeling structures, and constructing the amphitheater that bears the Wegeforth name.

Meanwhile, he had carried the dream of establishing a waterfront aquarium as a companion institution to the Zoo. He led in plans that brought the *Star of India,* an iron bark and last of the sailing ships to be operated commercially on the West Coast, to the San Diego waterfront as a maritime museum. But though he had donations promised to start work on the aquarium, he never reached agreement with city officials on a suitable location.

Until his death in 1941, he signed checks at the Zoo, intent on maintaining the sure knowledge of operations that he believed must be associated with the purse strings of any organization.

But also until his death, he fought the trend toward giving him personal publicity in the printed word for the work that he had done in building the Zoo. This was such a fetish that, in the twenties, the *San Diego Tribune* reported:

> The Lower Otay dam at the Zoo is 99% completed. The report was made by the San Diego Zoological Society and the language is that of a well-known physician and surgeon who objects to having his name in type except perhaps on certain types of more or less popular letterheads.

And in 1938, with an utterly spontaneous air, he sat down and wrote to C. A. McGrew, editor of the *San Diego Union,* this strange note:

Famed adventurers Martin and Osa Johnson were responsible for several popular animal additions to the San Diego Zoo.

Twenty-two years ago you advised that we use the name of Zoological Society in print so that it would become a society's function instead of an individual's. This counsel proved sound through the years, and every man on our board felt responsible for improvement and conduct in the Zoo. I am wondering if we could not continue in this same way. I noticed my name in your paper yesterday and I do not think it is a very healthy thing for the Zoo. Please have your reporters use merely the name of the Society.

He Traveled for His Family

Around the time that Lindbergh made his stirring flight across the Atlantic, Harry Wegeforth was hanging on desperately to the wing of a biplane over the Salton Sea, holding together a broken gas line while an unnerved pilot looked for a likely stretch of highway on which to make a forced landing.

Of course, he was on a Zoo mission. He'd chartered the plane to hunt for some white pelicans that had been seen around the Salton Sea in the Imperial Valley desert of Southern California. The pelicans waited for a later trip. He was fortunate to get back to San Diego alive, and he settled for that.

Belle Benchley joined the Zoo staff in 1926 and began to greatly assist Dr. Wegeforth. One of her jobs was the editorship of the monthly magazine ZOONOOZ.

In later years, he traveled to every continent in search of animals and plants to build his Zoo. During these trips he often risked his life as certainly as he had done over the Salton Sea; for most of them were made after his medical practice had been abandoned because of his heart attack, and his doctors had warned him against heat, altitude, and physical strain. His final trip, to India in 1940, led directly to his death.

Soon after establishment of the Zoo, he began his annual tours of the nation's zoos, studying their construction and operation, and swapping animals.

On the yacht of Captain Allan Hancock he made frequent excursions into Mexican and Alaskan waters. He even persuaded the United States Navy to take him seal hunting at Guadalupe Island, off Baja California.

After his heart attack in 1931, he began to make longer excursions. Aboard the *Velero III*, Captain Hancock's mammoth yacht, he and Cyrus Perkins, Zoo herpetologist, went

Dr. Wegeforth (saluting) and his companions during an expedition to the Galápagos Islands. The Velero III *(below) took "Doctor Harry" on many cruises. He poses (opposite) with Captain Allan Hancock and penguins on the deck of this ship on March 23, 1933.*

Photo courtesy of San Diego Historical Society.

to Ecuador in 1933 on an animal hunt. Two years later, he was off on his longest trip yet—to the Philippines and the Dutch East Indies. With him went penguins, mountain lions, and sea lions. Back with him, four months later, came rare Borneo orangutans, Philippine turtles, and the valued blue boar of the Celebes Island. Back, too, came 26 Gibbon apes, making the San Diego Zoo collection one of the outstanding ape collections of the world.

But ill health forced his return sooner than he had planned, and on the cruise homeward he already was planning his next trip to the Orient, where the animal markets and jungles fascinated him as surely as they would have fascinated the nine-year-old Harry Wegeforth with his backyard circus. Already he had given directions to Cyrus Perkins, his traveling companion, that if his heart finally collapsed during the trip, he should be cremated or buried at sea.

These were restless days for Harry Wegeforth. He knew that his time was nearly gone. While in San Diego, he drove hard and desperately for money and for construction so that his dream of a finished master Zoo could be attained before his death. But his nearness to the Zoo—and his constant daily hours there—seemed to provoke even greater heart strain and pain than his travels. A keen diagnostician—even of his own condition—he then would gather around him travel folders and atlases and plot his escape.

Through most of 1937, he held tickets for a trip around the world. His sailing was delayed until October 1937, by a long maritime strike. As he waited, he tramped about the Zoo during the day, directing workmen, overseeing every phase of operation; and during the evenings he read, or went to movies with his family, or listened to phonograph records.

But then he was off—sailing from San Pedro in a second-class cabin. With him went his cameras and bulky, hungry diaries in which he was to record with infinite detail every strange school of fish he sighted, every animal or bird he found in 29 zoos and countless animal markets, and a host of lore that for zoo people today would be considered an irreplaceable document of specialized information. His diaries soared over the 80,000-word mark before he returned to San Diego on June 3, 1938. He had visited zoos in Suva and Melbourne and Soerbaya and Calcutta and Cairo and Rome, Berlin and Hanover, Paris and London, Edinburgh and Kansas City. Back with him came 2,200 still photographs and 8,000 feet of movies, much of which has been preserved by his family. All along the way, he bought and traded animals that found their way to the San Diego Zoo by ship and freight during a period of many months.

No sooner was he back than he headed with Captain Hancock for a seal cruise off the northwest United States and Alaska.

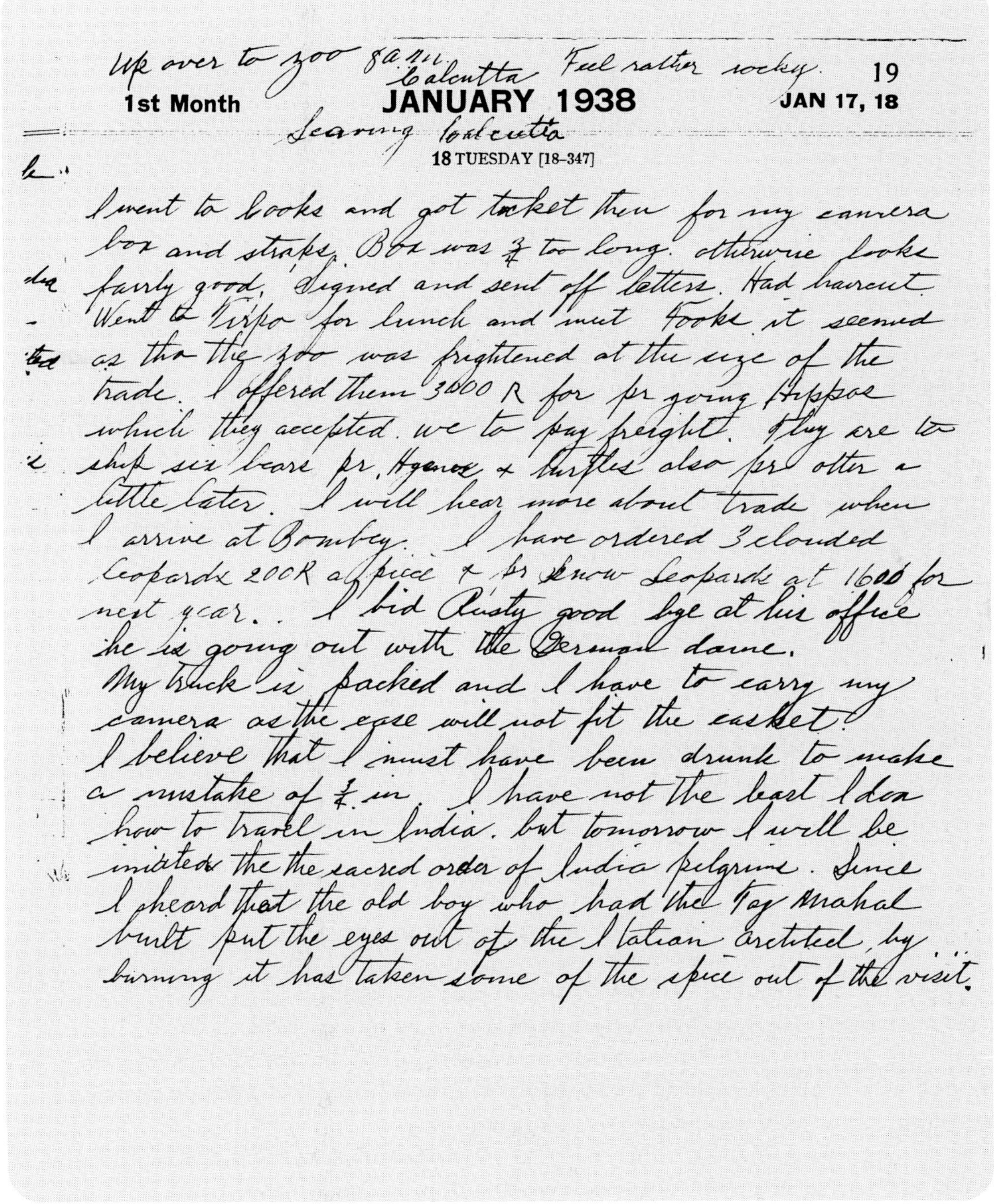

1st Month — **JANUARY 1938** — JAN 17, 18 — 19

Up over to zoo 8 a.m. Calcutta Feel rather rocky.

Leaving Calcutta

18 TUESDAY [18–347]

I went to Cooks and got ticket then for my camera box and straps. Box was ¾ too long. otherwise looks fairly good. Signed and sent off letters. Had haircut. Went to Firpo for lunch and met Cooke, it seemed as tho the zoo was frightened at the size of the trade. I offered them 3000 R for pr young Hippos which they accepted. we to pay freight. They are to ship six bears pr. Hyenas & turtles also pr otter a little later. I will hear more about trade when I arrive at Bombay. I have ordered 3 clouded leopards 200 R a piece & 3 Snow Leopards at 1600 for next year. I bid Rusty good bye at his office he is going out with the German dame.

My trunk is packed and I have to carry my camera as the case will not fit the casket! I believe that I must have been drunk to make a mistake of ¾ in. I have not the least idea how to travel in India. but tomorrow I will be initiated the the sacred order of India pilgrims. Since I pheard that the old boy who had the Taj Mahal built put the eyes out of the Italian architect, by burning it has taken some of the spice out of the visit.

A page from Dr. Wegeforth's diary, January 18, 1938, describes a day of animal trading in Calcutta.

On New Year's Day of 1939, he sailed aboard the *S.S. Brazil* from New York City for the east coast of South America, which he had not yet visited. His goal was a cruise up the Amazon and the Orinoco Rivers. He accomplished both, but his trip was a disappointment to him. Though he returned with 400 specimens for the Zoo, including two jaguars and many unusual snakes and birds, many of his prize specimens died during the long delays of transit. He met the Hancock yacht, *Velero III*, at Trinidad—and sailed back with Captain Hancock and his bride to San Diego, the decks of the yacht littered with cages bound for the Zoo.

It was during this cruise that his brother, Arthur, last of the three Wegeforth brothers to practice medicine in San Diego, passed away.

Ten months after his return, in April 1940, he sailed for the last time—to Saigon, Indo-China, and India. But the shadow of war was everywhere now. In Hong Kong, women and children were being evacuated in anticipation of the Japanese invasion. In Shanghai, he landed on the day that Marines captured Japanese officers who were carrying revolvers. In Calcutta, he was arrested for taking pictures on a bridge and his film confiscated.

Yet it was not war that stopped him finally, but bitter, twin attacks of pneumonia and malaria. He cancelled plans to go on to the Belgian Congo and booked passage back home to San Diego, depressed and gravely ill.

"It looks," he wrote, "as though we are getting squared away for a fight. It looks like we are going to be parading for the next generation. The only time I like to see soldiers is on a special day like Independence Day or Armistice Day. Outside of that I don't like to see them, because they always mean trouble."

And later:

"The only place left for me to go now is Australia, for there the war shadow is not yet reaching."

Despite his illness, on this last cruise, he ordered some 125 tropical Asiatic animals and 300 birds.

They were to be the last of his "family" that Harry Wegeforth personally adopted.

The "Check-In"

Amid a staff conference at the Zoo, Harry Wegeforth suddenly displayed the symptoms of suffocation and extreme pain so typical of the angina pectoris sufferer. As he grasped for a pill in his vest pocket, an aide rushed outside to the Zoo cafeteria and returned with a cup of strong coffee. He swallowed the pill with the coffee. Soon color began to return to his face and the pain was eased.

Then, the fortunes of the Zoo his obsession as always, he glared at the aide.

"Did you pay for that coffee?" he asked—and slapped down a nickel.

Dr. Wegeforth in his San Diego home. Left to right: son Milton, Rachel Wegeforth, and son Lester next to his father.

Harry Wegeforth did not fear death; he was only angered by the persistence of its threat. His letters during the final years often bore the phrase, "before I check in . . . ." He visited and wrote with Dr. Emil Novak, a University of Maryland classmate, and Dr. Milton J. Raisbeck, a New York City specialist. These letters show a humorous speculation over how long he might last, and a delighted spirit of revenge when he could report to them that he had made a forbidden trip and survived.

The last letter that he wrote in his life was to thank his old friend, Dr. Henry Harrower, then director of a pharmaceutical laboratory, for samples of a new heart drug that was giving him relief from the pain that then had become almost constant.

Yet no detail of the operation of his Zoo evaded him, to the last. Several days before his death, Zoo records show, he left a memorandum for Ralph Virden of the Zoo staff:

"I want the dirt left high in front of the dams in the canyons so that trucks when hauling dirt from other places can back over and dump it out."

When Belle Benchley left for a trip to the East in the spring of 1941, she remembers, Harry Wegeforth intimated that he would not be alive when she returned. He was not.

On June 24, 1941, he asked his friend and aide Joe Galvin to drive him to a tailor's for fittings of two new suits. When Galvin took him back to the family's comfortable home on Cypress Way in Marston Hills, Harry Wegeforth handed him some coins.

"Take these, Joe," he said. "This is the last tip you'll ever get from me."

Death came in the afternoon of the next day, with his wife and two sons at his side. Doctors said that he had avoided death with remarkable determination for an astonishing period of time.

His diaries show that he had extensive plans for new buildings at the Zoo and for modernization. But already, Martin Johnson, the famed wild animal collector, had termed the San Diego Zoo the finest on earth.

Because they knew it was what he would have ordered, Zoo employees—keepers, trainers, warehousemen, and clerks—worked at their tasks until half an hour before the funeral—and then came in a group, still dressed in their work uniforms. They heard the Reverend John B. Osborn say: "Doctor Harry loved and shared the language of flowers and all nature, and into his being was born a spiritual something. He gave more pleasure to little hearts and big hearts than any other person in California. He made education real, and his loving service to this city will be a lasting monument to his memory."

The *San Diego Union* credited him editorially as one of the ablest developers in San Diego history, a rare man who combined the talents of student and promoter. "He was as well known, perhaps," the newspaper stated, "in the animal markets of Africa, India, the Malay Peninsula and other remote areas as he was in San Diego."

Of him, the *San Diego Sun* had written: "The account of the Zoo's founding is one of the most impressive stories of disinterested public service that San Diego or any other city may boast."

His son Milton, carrying out a wish of the Zoo founder, accepted appointment to the board of directors of the San Diego Zoological Society shortly after the death of Harry Wegeforth and has retained that affiliation ever since. An annual "free day" at the Zoo—when no admission is charged—has been established in memory of Harry Wegeforth.

But to the thousands who knew him, the memory of Harry Wegeforth that they hold most dear is that of the man who led them excitedly over the acres of the San Diego Zoo and stopped to show them a kangaroo who was having wife trouble, or an old lady elephant who wouldn't go near the water, or a polar bear who liked to have his back scratched.

For these were his "family."

PART TWO

STORIES OF THE ZOO

by Dr. Harry M. Wegeforth

The San Diego Zoo's plaque of founders includes the names of three additional men besides Wegeforth and his brother Paul.

CHARTER MEMBERS OF THE ZOOLOGICAL SOCIETY AND FOUNDERS OF THE SAN DIEGO ZOOLOGICAL GARDEN.

HARRY M. WEGEFORTH. M.D PRES
PAUL WEGEFORTH. M.D SEC.
FRED BAKER. M.D
JOSEPH H. THOMPSON. M.D TRES.
FRANK S STEPHENS

A Zoo is Born

On September 16, 1916, as I was returning to my office after performing an operation at the St. Joseph Hospital, I drove down Sixth Avenue and heard the roaring of the lions in the cages at the Exposition then being held in Balboa Park.

I turned to my brother, Paul, who was riding with me, and half jokingly, half wishfully, said, "Wouldn't it be splendid if San Diego had a zoo! You know . . . I think I'll start one." Taking me at my word, he replied that he would be glad to help me but added dubiously that he did not see how such a project could be put over on the heels of an Exposition not very successful in its second year.

I had long nurtured the thought of a San Diego Zoo and now—suddenly—I decided to try to establish one. Dropping my brother at our office, I went down to the *San Diego Union* where I talked long and earnestly with Mr. Clarence McGrew, the city editor. Next morning, the following article appeared in the Union, prominently featured:

SAN DIEGO ZOO
PLAN OF ANIMAL LIFE STUDENTS
May form Society to Support
Large Collection.

Drs. Harry M. and Paul Wegeforth are interested in the promotion of a zoological society for San Diego, which will have for its object the development and support of a zoological garden to be maintained out of the funds that the society will raise through dues and subscriptions.

There are a number of physicians and scientists such as Drs. Baker, Thompson, Gregg and Archie Talboy in this city and county, who are interested in the study of animal life and it is proposed to combine them in a nucleus which will later be developed into an efficient organization.

"We already have a good start," said Dr. Harry Wegeforth, "in the collection we have at the Exposition. The cost of maintaining these animals is not large.

"There are tons of animals from Mexico, Central and South America coming through our port and being distributed among cities like Chicago, New York and San Francisco. These animals are gifts. Why can't we keep some of them here? The zoological societies trade animals with each other and we can do the same thing when we get a surplus of any one species."

The response was instantaneous and gratifying. Dr. Fred Baker, a practicing physician with a strong zoological bent, telephoned and offered his assistance. Dr. J. H. Thompson, a commander in the medical division of the Navy, called at my office, eager to be of help. We commandeered Mr. Frank Stephens of the Natural History Society, and thus our Board of Directors was born—these three men, my brother Paul, and myself.

Our fledgling board of directors held an informal meeting in Paul's and my offices in the Granger Building and set the first official meeting of the Board of Directors of the San Diego Zoological Society for October 2 at the home of Dr. Baker. The New York Zoological Society was the most outstanding in the country. We obtained copies of their by-laws and constitution to serve as a model, held our first official meeting, and the San Diego Zoological Society was launched.

On November 24, Mr. Horton L. Titus, Paul's friend and mine, who did all the early legal work of the Zoo, presented the articles of incorporation to the Board of Directors. They were submitted to Mayor Capps and to George W. Marston, president of the Board of Park Commissioners, signed by both and sent to the State for incorporation. Armed with the dignity of a corporation, we started to work in earnest.

Our first problem was to select a location. We decided to petition the Board of Park Commissioners for Pepper Grove in Balboa Park, a popular picnic ground planted with drooping pepper trees. The grove was too small for our purposes, but we proceeded on the theory that he who asks less gets more. Besides, we felt comfortably assured that the Board would not let us have it—for the noise from the Zoo animals would have a most discordant and disastrous effect upon concerts given in the organ pavilion nearby.

Sundry small collections of animals dotted the park; one small zoo brought in by the Exposition company ranged along Park Boulevard; another tiny zoo consisted of buffalo and deer and a pair of bears, located on the west side of the park, south of the approach to Laurel Street Bridge; on 6th Street near Juniper stood a cage of ducks donated to the park by Joseph Sefton, Jr.; then in the Pepper Grove there was a herd of Panama deer, and south of the organ pavilion, a herd of elk.

The Board of Park Commissioners granted us supervision over most of these animals. Local newspapers were generous with publicity and, as a result, a thin stream of animals began dribbling in. Numerous small animals came in from individuals pleased by the thought of a San Diego Zoo. As they were donated to us, we would place them in the group to which they were most nearly related.

One of our first donations was a massive female bear misnamed Caesar. Dr. Thompson of our Board of Directors was attached to the Marines and the captain of a Navy ship presented the bear to him. It had been a pet on the boat and was fondled and made much of by the sailor boys in the crew. However, Caesar had a one-track mind and when she started down a passageway on the boat, regardless of who was in the way—it made no difference whether admiral or third-class gob, for Caesar was a real democrat—she kept going. She was as large as a good-sized pig and generally ended up by having the passageway to herself. This is the true story, as bedtime stories have it, of why Caesar was ousted from the Navy under a cloud.

We scratched our heads, wondering how to get her to the Zoo. None of us knew

Dr. Harry M. Wegeforth is seen in this formal portrait at about the time the San Diego Zoo was founded. He would later state that "The whole Zoo was a gamble from the start. . . ."

anything about crating bears nor did we have a truck or even the money to rent a truck. We did the only thing we could—put a collar and chain around Caesar's neck and seated her beside Dr. Thompson in the front seat of his auto. As the citizenry gaped, the two of them drove through the city to the Zoo, which was then just a few cages left from the Exposition, little more than Menagerie Row.

The Kodiak grew like a weed. As the 21st Army Infantry camp was located close to the Zoo, Caesar had plenty of food, for anything that would eat garbage was assured of being amply fed. She soon outgrew her pet stage. She did not like her cage and expressed her disapproval by wrecking it repeatedly. We would find her in one pen one day and in another the next. When we found two-inch planks would not hold her and she snapped 2 x 4s like toothpicks, we covered the woodwork with heavy sheet metal, and at last we were satisfied that our worries were over. But Caesar had just begun to fight! She ripped this off like cardboard and then we realized that no longer could we postpone the construction of a new grotto.

Somehow—I can't remember where, except that much of the money was donated by Zoo fans who wanted to see the animals in surroundings resembling their native

The infamous bear grotto that had to be redone with a concrete floor to prevent the bears from tunneling.

habitat—we raised about $2,200 and began the grotto which still stands today, the one backing on Alameda Street. Mr. T. M. Russell, a prominent contractor, now of our Board of Directors, was selected to build the structure. We realized that this was not enough to complete the grotto as we would have liked, and so decided to dispense with a concrete floor and let the ground suffice. We built the wall deep into the ground and separated the animals with wire fencing. When the grotto was ready, we moved Caesar, a black bear, and a polar bear in, under the beaming gaze of enthusiastic zoo members. Then we all went home, sure our Rubicon was behind us.

Next morning on my way to the hospital, at peace with the world, I stopped once more to look at the grottoes. My serenity vanished like a dewdrop on a griddle when I saw what Caesar had done—something we could not have duplicated without dynamite. She must have worked furiously all through the night, for deep into the earth underneath the wall she had dug a huge tunnel—big enough for a small truck to drive through. Chunks of concrete reinforcing the back of the grotto had been thrown around like alphabet blocks. Dirt was heaped up high next to the wire fencing and Caesar had mounted this and was now making the acquaintance of the polar bear. (They were getting along amicably, and this first gave me the idea of combining the varieties of bears in one grotto, which we later practiced.)

The bears' sleeping quarters were under the walk of the bear pit, divided by steel rods. We enticed Caesar and the polar bear in with food and locked the door. The black bear was driven in without much difficulty. No sooner did we have them all safely in, than Caesar sat down and methodically began to pull and bend the steel rods. I telephoned the iron company hurriedly about it. She couldn't possibly injure those rods, they assured me—but when the company man saw what she had done, they immediately installed heavy gratings left from some jail construction work and fixed them firmly on the outside. They remained there for many years, reminding me of Caesar's spectacular development from a frolicsome pet to the Goliath of the Zoo.

There was no more compromising about a concrete floor! Caesar's excavating proclivities settled that. Miss Ellen Scripps gave us the first donation. Our original idea had been a native-habitat project, but since then we had become interested in the possibilities of the moat design. A wall was built at the edge of the road where visitors stood. Then came the moat. Next, the floor of the grotto was built up considerably higher than the front. The low wall where visitors stood was built up so that, to the average person's eye, it would seem to be on a level with the floor of the grotto; thus, the bear standing on the grotto would appear—from a distance—to be standing on the front wall.

So successfully was this accomplished, that for years afterwards every Sunday we had a stream of people running to the office excitedly telling us the bears were out. As one turned around the O'Rourke Building and looked back at the bear pit, the effect of the bears appearing to stand on the wall was convincing enough!

One bright, sunny day we had a genuine case of loose bear. A sailor had brought in a nice pet bear grown so large he was no longer considered a respectable mascot for a Navy boat. His claws were very sharp. He didn't like the unaccustomed company of so many bears, so he simply scaled over some sixteen feet of wall! When we went out to investigate this latest "escaped" animal rumor, we found him surrounded by twenty or thirty children, happy to be the single cynosure for human affection and joyously swallowing handfuls of popcorn and candy fed him by delighted children.

How to Kidnap an Alligator

Part of the animals in the Exposition group came from the old menagerie at Wonderland, Ocean Beach, which had gone broke. They had been brought to San Diego by a Mr. Kaufman, together with some animals of his own, and the Exposition company rented the lot for forty dollars a day. The lone keeper was a one-armed man (hence called "Army") with an inordinate fondness for hard liquor.

We had only the proverbial shoestring with which to carry on. However, the only group of animals we had to buy immediately was the rented one. The rest we could let

The Zoo's bears, like these two early residents, have always been a popular exhibit.

ride, for the Board of Park Commissioners was taking care of them—albeit reluctantly.

I approached Mr. Carl Heilbron, who, I believe, was chairman of the trustees of the defunct Wonderland Company, about purchasing these animals. They offered us the group for six thousand dollars. We learned that most of the animals were claimed by Mr. Kaufman, and there followed another series of huddles with the trustees, until they agreed to take $2,500 for all they could give us clear title to. We paid them $500—and in the end they made us a gift of the $2,000 balance for they would have had to board the animals until we paid it off.

Along with the animals, we adopted Army. For food we used horses. Through a curious paradox, the price of hides had risen sharply because of the war but we could purchase horses for practically nothing. So we fed the meat to the animals and sold the hides for $5 or $6, thus bringing in enough revenue to pay Army's meager salary.

One of the animals that came to us in the Wonderland Zoo contingent was an old and rheumy hyena. This poor, miserable creature appeared to be suffering grievously and was such a horrible looking specimen that, beyond a doubt, its fate was death. However, our exhibit was small and this was the only hyena on the Pacific Coast so we kept putting off the day when he would be put down.

From time to time the hyena showed slight improvement but invariably would backslide and resume his previous wasted appearance. One day as I was making my rounds, he seemed gaunter, bonier, and more wretched than ever so I gave firm orders that he must be killed.

The next day a man from a Hollywood film company called on me. His company was producing a picture depicting the horrendous effects wrought by the use of opiates; a well-known star had died from an overdose of morphine and his wife was to appear in the picture. He wound up saying they were in search of a hyena to be used in the fade-outs personifying the tortured spirits of narcotics addicts.

As soon as he got to the point, I rushed him over to the monkey cages that then housed other animals, as we did not have enough monkeys to fill them. No hyena was to be seen and I called loudly to one of the men to drive him out, fervently hoping he was not already dead. The hyena walked out towards us, but my heart sank for he was the most terrible looking object I have ever seen. The moving picture agent's face lighted up delightedly, however, and he crowed, "Wonderful! He's just what we wanted. He couldn't have been better." He gave us $200 for the animal, which as I realized when I became wiser in the ways of the motion-picture world, was much less than he was worth to them. But to us it was found money, and besides he would never have survived the week, I am sure.

When the picture came to San Diego, I made a point of seeing it. There was our hyena, looking appropriately gruesome and frightful, fading into various scenes and fading out again, sending horror-laden shudders down the audience's spine.

So the hyena was our first animal to break into the movies. Since then a great many of our exhibits have followed the steps of their cadaverous predecessor into films.

Now, however, the problem of finances hung over us more ominously than ever for we had to pay for the animals and meet the innumerable expenses constantly arising. We emerged from another meeting of the Board of Directors with a plan for life memberships and, inside of three or four days, had raised about a thousand dollars in memberships at two hundred dollars apiece. Mr. George W. Marston, Mr. Paul Granger, Mr. Roy Howard, and Mr. Joseph Sefton all became life members at this time. Mr. George Champlin was taken in to promote memberships and soon we could count a hundred and twenty members. Taking inventory of ourselves, we felt we had achieved noteworthy status as a budding zoological society possessing a collection of animals—however fragmentary—and a fair-sized membership list for an infant society.

In the early part of 1917, through the inspiration of W. H. Porterfield of the *San Diego Sun*, the Junior San Diego Zoological Society was conceived. The purpose was a better reciprocal relationship with the children of San Diego; to make our Zoo a more integral, intimate and enriching contribution to their lives, and in return to secure their support for the Zoo—have them grow up with us, as it were. From the Zoo's inception, the role it should assume in the lives of San Diego's children had been a paramount concern.

Duncan McKinnon, superintendent of the Board of Education, greeted the plan enthusiastically. With his cooperation and to the accompaniment of copious newspaper publicity, we were soon in the midst of a campaign to roll up a large membership for our Junior Zoological Society, charging a nominal fifty-cent fee.

About this time, Dr. Thompson began to feel that we should tie in more educational work with the Zoo and concluded with a decision to deliver lectures at the cages of our animals on Park Boulevard. Two o'clock one Saturday afternoon was the date for the first lecture, and we awaited this dubiously to see what the response would be. Saturday morning it began to drizzle and by two o'clock the rain was streaming inexorably down. Our doubts resolved into black pessimism; we drove by the grounds to see whether a hardy straggler or two had shown up. To our delight, about fifty intrepid and umbrellaed people were standing in the rain, waiting for the lecture. Dr. Thompson gave me a triumphant look, climbed out of the car, and launched into an excellent address.

These Saturday afternoon talks became so successful that we expanded into nature walks and later into other natural history subjects.

After the Exposition closed, we began to look for a building to house the Zoo staff, although we still did not know where the Zoo would be nor were we certain there would be a Zoo. The Standard Oil Building erected as an Exposition exhibit on Alameda Street (just opposite where the Zoo is now) we thought would be ideal. Mr. E. G. Sykes, then superintendent of the Standard Oil Company, had come from Franklin, Pennsylvania, where my father had been in the oil business so I utilized this paternal approach. He had been planning to tear down the building and use the lumber for a garage, but at length consented to give it to us. This was an enormous gift for our budding Zoo. I look back upon this as my maiden exploit in securing sizable donations—which of course have provided one of the chief means of maintaining and expanding the Zoo.

But now came a stumbling block. The City Attorney advised us that the Zoological Society could not own buildings but suggested that the building be given to the Park Department for the use of the Zoological Society. This was done.

Still the question of where to put the Zoo hung fire, and we struggled along as best we could, endeavoring to get the Board of Park Commissioners to assign us a home. They recommended the present site of the Zoo as preferable to Pepper Grove, but it was a recommendation and nothing more. Then in the spring the United States entered the World War. Dr. Thompson was ordered elsewhere immediately. I volunteered, having just turned 35, but was rejected, for in October, 1916, I had had an appendectomy. Probably it was a lucky turn of affairs for the Zoo that the Army could not use me then

A new cage for eagles draws visitor attention in 1923. Below, enclosures for hoofed stock under construction in May of 1922.

for in these early days there was a tremendous lot of work to do and very few people to do it. My medical work at the office had increased greatly, and as practically all of the superintending of the Zoo was in my lap, the Trojan of the adage had nothing on me.

In May 1917, after months of negotiating, the Board of Park Commissioners decided to turn the land from Alameda Drive to the 11th Street Canyon over to us. Then they found they could not give us the land without a vote of the people. (By this time, we were learning that, politically speaking, a straight line is by no means the shortest distance between two points!) This, too, was taken up with the City Attorney, and he advised us that the best solution would be to transfer the ownership of the animals to the City of San Diego; then the Zoological Society would not legally own either the land or the animals but would be the administrative body for the Zoo, retaining the right to sell or trade whatever surplus animals we deemed unnecessary for exhibition.

In 1910, on Third Street between Broadway and E on the east side of the street stood an old wooden stable which a Mr. Cordtz used as headquarters for his billboard concern. Here he kept a miniature zoo, including coons, coatimundis, an alligator, and fish.

When the Plaza and Cabrillo theaters went up, the stable came down and Mr. Cordtz moved to a house just east of 30th Street, then a pretty much isolated district. In his yard he had a pool constructed for the lone seven-foot alligator. Then, for some reason he closed up his house, disposed of most of his animals, and moved out of the city—leaving the alligator, who promptly developed a roving disposition. Frequently he would go for a little stroll (or whatever the reptilian equivalent is) but would faithfully return to the pool.

At this time, a professional colleague of mine (who shall be nameless) and I were performing an operation together. The reason is obscure now—but we decided to do something about the perambulating alligator. We contacted Mr. Cordtz but he was adamant, refusing to sell it or to dispose of it in any way.

Two gentlemen of our mettle were not so easily thwarted, however.

A few days later this physician and his wife came over to spend the evening at my home. Irresistibly the conversation turned to the alligator, and a few minutes later found us driving in the bright moonlight to the pool where the alligator lived. We roped the astonished creature and dragged her into an oblong, coffinlike box that had been prepared with malice aforethought. We lifted the bound victim onto the back of the car. Then we tied a rope around her neck and secured it so it would not choke her but also so that she could not wriggle out of it.

We were an excited dinner party as we hurried through the meal and then went out to gloat rather nervously over our prey. She had now maneuvered herself farther out from the box, and a grotesque picture she made with her front feet grasping its edge and her gaunt and horny head thrust high up in the moonlight.

HOW TO KIDNAP AN ALLIGATOR

What a lot of vigorous pushing and pulling it took to get that alligator back into the box! Then we drove across the city to the park near Laurel Street and the Sixth Avenue approach to the bridge spanning the 11th Street canyon, where a pair of bears and a few buffalo comprised the municipal Zoo.

Well in the shadows and with our ears alert for the sound of approaching footsteps, we tugged until we got the box unloaded, lifted out the alligator and tied her to a tree. Then back to town we drove, filled with a mixture of guilt and civic pride.

I stopped at a pay telephone, and pitching my voice to a deep bass, called up the local papers and told them the story of this "wild beast" in the park. The reporters—a cynical lot—dismissed it as a gag, laughed at me patronizingly, and refused to go down to verify it. The next day they had to swallow some of their callow disbelief, for the alligator was found and then both papers played up the story of its extraordinary appearance. The Board of Park Commissioners, finding itself suddenly the none-too-pleased owners of a mysterious alligator, had a small pool dug for it, and this strange new acquisition soon became the park's most popular exhibit.

I was to find that the way of the transgressor is hard, or at least highly uncomfortable. The day following the abduction of the alligator, William Moore, claims adjustor for the Spreckels Electric Company and a crony of mine, phoned me and asked me to be present

A portion of Zoo grounds called Alligator Canyon. The plan was to build a dam here and flood it for an alligator enclosure.

when he interviewed the witness of an accident in which his clients were involved. To my discomposure, the witness turned out to be Mr. Cordtz!

Not realizing he was addressing one of the culprits, Mr. Cordtz launched into an eloquent description of what he would do to the scoundrels who stole his alligator if he ever caught them. He had learned of the event in the newspapers, and though he said he didn't want the creature back, he evidenced an unwholesome zest for vengeance. I was perfectly willing to close the chapter and change the subject—but not so Mr. Moore. No sooner would Mr. Cordtz' dire threats abate a bit than Mr. Moore would pose another question about the alligator. Somewhere, somehow, it was obvious that he had learned more than he had read in the papers, and I was in a pretty feverish state when I finally managed to escape.

Whenever I met Mr. Cordtz he would describe in great detail a plan he had to catch the thieves and say he expected to get them before long. Of course I avoided him whenever possible, but he knew I liked animals and looked me up with unquenching frequency. I developed a permanent little chill down my spine from the thought of what would happen if he ever discovered the identity of the robbers.

When in 1917 the Zoological Society acquired the little group of animals on the west side of the park, the alligator accompanied them. Then we learned with accuracy that she was a female. For years she remained the only female in our collection, although a shipment of about half a dozen large alligators sent us by General and Mrs. M. O. Terry from Florida was supposed to contain several—a supposition unsubstantiated by nature. For several years in succession, she laid eggs and built a mound over them as alligators do in their native habitat, but always the rats devoured them before they could be incubated. This aged female is still with us, and though I cannot face her without reminiscent qualms, I believe we did the humane thing in removing her to the park. She has been well cared for, and I am sure that if she had stayed in the 30th Street pool, sooner or later she would have injured some of the children in the neighborhood.

A Home at Last

About the middle of 1917, our Zoo underwent one of the recurrent little crises that still continue to punctuate its never-too-placid existence. The 21st Army Infantry was located on the site of the present Roosevelt School. The slaughterhouse for our horses stood just south of the present Indian Village—about 200 yards from the camp. This proximity was unwelcome to the Army officers; their medical staff visited the grounds of our abattoir, inspected it, and condemned it. Today such a contingency would be only one more complication in the day's affairs, but then it was a major calamity. After a succession of conferences with the Colonel, the medical officers, etc., in which we rose to diplomatic heights, we

Mirror Lagoon in 1922, as photographed from the roof of the Harvester Building. Monkey Quadrangle is in the background. Below, a view across the canyon at the MacRae Cages (lining the hill) with the large Scripps Flight Cage behind them.

A portion of Dr. Wegeforth's Zoo office displaying many of his travel trophies. Opposite, the Board Room.

remodeled the building, following closely the requirements of the medical board until at last, with a sigh, we heard them give their consent to allow our abattoir to remain there.

When the United States entered the war, the nation had little time for frivolity and within a few months practically all circuses had disbanded. One small circus that happened to be in San Diego when war was declared had four young lions. We already had nine, but I gave a note for $50 for the four young cubs and added them to our colony. By that happy horse-and-hide paradox mentioned before, the more meat-eating animals we had, the easier it became to pay the salary of the keeper and the food bills for nonmeat-eating animals; because every time a horse was slaughtered for food (and often these were given to us), we gleaned $6 or $7 for the hide.

I cannot remember a time in the early days of the Zoo when we were not in financial straits, and every so often these reached hazardous peaks. One evening I sat in the reading room of the Elks Club mulling over means of conjuring up a nice, big lump of money.

"Hello," I heard a voice greet me, "compared to you Job must have looked like a playboy. What's the trouble?"

George Brown and Otto Jensen stood at my elbow. I was glad to pour my troubles into sympathetic ears. They suggested putting on a show. We ended by deciding on a field meet between the Marines and the Navy.

The United States had embarked on a program of preparedness at that time, and no sooner had we begun arrangements for the meet than a government committee appointed to investigate fund-raising activities that might conflict with preparedness projects demanded that we abandon it.

There were three men on the committee, and as one of them was hostile to the Zoo, *finis* might have been written across our meet had it not been for Mr. M. C. Pfefferkorn, vice president of the First National Trust & Savings Bank and an influential local figure. He, together with several other men interested in athletics, appeared before the committee; after a good deal of tall and fancy talking, we convinced the committee that our show would not appreciably cut the receipts of any military or Red Cross affairs, and they permitted us to proceed with our plans.

About a week before the meet, Otto Jensen left to take a job in the north; five days later George Brown was called to Mexico. This left me feeling a little like a bantam hen who finds she has hatched an ostrich. However, George helped me as much as he could before he left, and Mr. Pfefferkorn agreed to take charge of the field events with the help of several friends from the YMCA.

Saturday, October 6, the day of the meet, dawned bright and clear. As the hour to open the gates approached, the men who had promised to take tickets were nowhere to be seen. Dr. Baker took one gate and I took the other until I could draft somebody to relieve me. The admission was only 10 cents, but as the people poured through the gates, our receipts soared to a very gratifying figure.

The prizes were half a dozen boxes of cigars donated by Mr. Sensenbrenner, a San Diego cigar manufacturer. The winning contestants so far outnumbered the boxes that we had to open them up and dole them out, two-for-a-prize.

The venture was highly successful, and we all breathed easier as the Zoo acquired a new lease on life.

Three or four months after I had been rejected by the Army, I reapplied to the Medical Board. In July 1918, orders came to report for service. I resigned from the Board of Directors as President and Joseph Sefton, Jr. was appointed to succeed me.

In January 1919, I returned to civilian life. My medical clientele demanded more than normal attention after my absence. As for the Zoo, this was no lotus eater's pastime; it monopolized whatever leisure I had from my practice. One of my principal worries was our pot-valiant keeper and the fact that we had no one to replace him should he drink himself into irresponsibility. Eventually I let him go and hired Jack Hendee, who had been in charge of the Zoo at Universal City. Jack was a much better attendant and, furthermore, handled the new members who came up to see their Zoo with considerably more tact.

It was only by a sort of careful prestidigitation that we could meet our maintenance costs and there was little or nothing left for the purchase of animals. To many of the people donating them we gave yearly memberships. One of the very few we bought was a pair of opossums, for which we paid $2.50. We laugh at that now for the county is so overrun with opossums that almost every day sees several brought into the Zoo window by harassed citizens.

Every now and then we would be offered donations of animals that we couldn't afford to refuse but whose upkeep would have constituted an outsize liability. One firm notified us to buy a pair of grizzly bears and they would pay the cost. We had our hands more than full with the Kodiak bear and were not in the market for any more trouble just then. Eventually we got around that problem by taking the generous donation but did not order the bears until several years later.

Along about May and October, I often went to New York in connection with my medical practice, and always made the most of the opportunity to visit animal dealers. One memorable day, in a dealer's backyard I saw a harpy eagle and another rare vulture. The dealer, not realizing what they were, sold them to me for $75. From there I went on to the Bronx Zoo, where the envious director told me he had a standing order at $250 each for any of these birds that appeared on the market.

Each trip that a member of the Board made to the East—or almost anywhere—meant something new for the Zoo. Thus we were able to keep our exhibits fresh and interesting and not too much of a twice-told tale to the public.

The herd of elk roaming back of the organ pavilion had increased to 24 by 1919. These had been brought in by the Supervisors for the Exposition. The expense of maintaining two dozen elk was a constant drain on our anemic treasury and I quailed as I contemplated their propensity for multiplying. At last, with the consent of the Board of Park Commissioners, we interested the San Diego Elks Lodge in transferring half of them to the Cleveland National Forest, Laguna Mountains, where they thoroughly justified our qualms, increasing until at one time 64 were counted.

In August 1921, the matter of a location for our Zoo again came before the Board of Park Commissioners, and we were granted some 150 acres of the present 200-acre Zoo. This excluded a good-sized portion of the present deer mesa, which was occupied by an auto camp. Then, in September, I appeared before the Board and asked that the grounds and building maintained by the International Harvester Company be annexed. This, too, was granted. Our Board of Directors had spent a great deal of time studying the most important zoological gardens in the country and consulting the most eminent men in this line, including Dr. Hornaday of the Bronx Zoo and Mr. Hagenbeck. In November, we presented a landscape map and our plans showing proposed disposition of corrals, cages, and dens to the Board of Park Commissioners, and these were approved without dissent. At last, early in 1922, we began to move into our new quarters.

From the first I was struck by the marvelous potential of the grounds, with its mesas and canyons, for development into a capacious, sylvan zoo. As animals were acquired, quarters were built in the mesas and canyons with this picture in mind, instead of merely adding buildings in a row. Although in the beginning some of the animals seemed fantastically far apart, I'm sure that a "Gallup poll" of our visitors would substantiate that our original plan has fully vindicated itself.

A luxuriant growth of trees and foliage was one of the chief features of the Zoo as I planned it in my mind's eye. Our first tree-planting attempts met with sad ends. Being amateurs and not having a gardener, many of our trees died. As soon as the few hardy survivors attained a little growth, they were attacked by a swarm of boys who would climb them and make the branches sway until they broke. Practically all the trees we planted were destroyed this way before we were able to break up the gang of boys who committed the vandalism.

Thumbing over the newspaper clippings and publicity of the Zoo's tender first years, I recollect the unceasing work it took to keep the Zoo always in the public eye and to make San Diego zoo-minded. The editors of the three local papers, Mr. James MacMullen, Mr. C. A. McGrew, and Mr. W. H. Porterfield, acted as an advisory committee on publicity. They gave us liberal space in their papers and a wealth of invaluable advice. Through all the years of the Zoo's life, the generosity and cooperation of the newspaper editors has never flagged, and I believe they deserve a great deal of the credit for building up the San Diego Zoo.

Elephants Cause Headaches

Elephants were such a vital part of our animal collection, and their possession has been accompanied by so many colorful incidents, that I feel they have earned a chapter to themselves.

The story of how we acquired our first elephants reminds me of the fictional foreign newspaper correspondent who reported a battle and then had to make one to justify his account. We had told the public—with much fanfare and on several different occasions—that we were getting elephants and then had to make good.

One morning James MacMullen of the *Union* telephoned me to ask if we wanted a pair of elephants, that the Sells Floto Circus was coming to town and would donate them to the Zoo if the newspapers would handle their publicity gratis. A few minutes later, Mr. Porterfield of the *Sun* called with a similar message.

What marvelous news for the Zoo! With high heart, I thanked them and the publicity was started.

At last the great day arrived. The mayor, our congressman, Mr. John D. Spreckels and a collection of other prominent San Diegans promised to attend the afternoon show so that the presentation would be witnessed in proper style. Admiral Burridge, who was in charge of the fleet here then, consented to accept the elephants for us.

The trained horse was the last act. Then the band was to play the Star Spangled Banner and Admiral Burridge was to march out and receive the elephants. Well . . . the horse did his act, the band played . . . but there was no sign of an elephant. A desolate pall settled on the two hundred people in the Zoo section as the rest of the crowd began to flood out the doorways.

A lawyer in our party advised us to drop the matter because it would be costlier and more troublesome to drag the case through the courts—and still with no assurance that we would get the elephants—than to raise money to buy some. Disappointed and disgusted,

Dr. Wegeforth rides one of the Zoo's first elephants. A great deal of difficulty accompanied the Zoo's efforts to obtain these animals.

several of our fans offered to buy the elephants, but the Sells Floto people would not even listen and offered no apology or explanation beyond denying that they had ever been a party to the alleged elephants-for-publicity deal. Two possible explanations occur to me: an overly enthusiastic publicity man had committed the circus to something it couldn't deliver, or a matter that had begun as a joke had gotten pretty thoroughly out of hand.

So, as it turned out, the Zoological Society's first elephants never attained real flesh-and-blood status.

Next week the Ringling Circus came to town, John Ringling with it. The brothers, John and Charles, were good friends of mine and normally I would have looked him up as soon as he arrived, but just then I was a little sensitive about circuses. The morning of the show, a Mr. Hathaway dropped in on me, sent by John Ringling, and I promised to be there for the afternoon show.

With reluctant feet, I went down to the grounds and met Mr. Ringling between the menagerie and the big tent. We chatted for a quarter of an hour, dozens of people passing by. Every few minutes one of my acquaintances would call out with misplaced wit, "Getting another elephant, Doc?" and "What kind of elephant did you get this time?" At last

Mr. Ringling asked why they were riding me, and I unbosomed myself. He promptly called his elephant man and asked if they could spare an elephant.

"There's Albert," the keeper replied. Albert, it seemed, was a bull they were keeping in the car because he was in musth [rutting season]. Mr. Ringling turned to me and said we could have Albert. Coming up with a bound out of my despondence, I asked that he present him to Admiral Burridge at dinner that night and we could notify the newspapers.

Like the horse act and the national anthem on the previous occasion, the dinner went off beautifully.

But when it came to getting Albert out of the car, he proved he had a mind of his own. We tried every conceivable stratagem and force but Albert merely sat. Finally at 1:00 a.m., we confessed ourselves beaten and gave up. Shuddering at the thought of being the butt again, I phoned the newspaper to kill the story. "Too late," they said, for the paper went to press at 2:00. So they inserted an "almost" after the caption, and the paper went out to thousands of San Diego homes reading "The Zoo Receives an Elephant—Almost."

Mr. Ringling was almost as disappointed as we were. The next day we had a two-page wire from him vowing that we should have our elephants, that he would bring us some on his next trip to the coast. Actually, our first elephants came in 1923, from India, through the efforts of Frank Buck.

Half a dozen zoo superintendents had told me that when I got my elephants I would acquire with them one long, continuous headache, and this was no overstatement. We hired a baggage car to bring our animals down from San Francisco. The elephants (who were called Empress and Queenie) were led into one end of the car and the rest of the animals into the other, and two of the Zoo employees clambered in with them. As soon as the elephants found themselves boarded in, they started on a mad rampage, trying to yank out the bars across the windows and wreck the car.

Somewhat to my surprise, the car pulled into San Diego without any dire mishap. Here the switch engine was attached and the signal cord to the engine hooked up. The car had gone only a few hundred yards when the elephants grabbed the signal cord and gave such eccentric signals that the engineer stopped the car short in alarm, almost throwing the elephants on their heads and staggering the men in the car with them.

We placed a heavy sheet of iron between the car and the unloading platform and the elephants walked over that meekly. Then, they evidently decided they had been pushed around enough since their long trip from India, with all its strange, bewildering experience, and so they staged a stand-up strike—just stood there, immovable. Chains had been put on their legs so they couldn't move too far in the wrong direction—an utterly unnecessary precaution. We pushed and we pulled with an elephant hook, but staunch as Gibralter they remained.

At last it occurred to me that they probably were accustomed to being ridden. Ready to resort to anything now, I climbed up on Empress and found that by kicking her on the side of the head I could get her to move, and could get her to go in the direction I wanted by pushing with the hook in back of her ear or pulling backwards from the front of the ear. Harry Edwards, one of the men from the Zoo, mounted Queenie and found the same code worked. Then we had the chains taken off their legs. Feeling like Indian rajahs and also pretty silly, we rode on through the city. More than one driver slammed on his brakes in a hurry when he saw those huge animals looming out of the dark on the familiar streets of San Diego.

As we neared the Zoo, the many members of the Zoological Society who had gathered to welcome the new exhibits witnessed our regal entrance. Just inside the Zoo, the elephants balked again. This time we did not urge them too much, for the poor beasts must have had an even more exhausting and nerve-wracking day than we had. Eventually, however, they were settled in their new quarters, consumed a hearty supper, and I drew the first tranquil breath I had enjoyed in 24 hours.

Not long after that, Mr. Ringling wired saying the circus would soon be in San Diego again and the promised elephants would come back with them. Frank Buck was then working for us and, without consulting me, wired back declining the elephants and asking for other animals instead! I was dumbfounded when I learned about this on the circus' arrival—hardly adequate thanks for Mr. Ringling's trouble in transporting them across the continent for us. Of course, they did not carry a sideline of animals around with them like spare tires, but they did give us a tiger, a zebra, and a camel.

My next problem was money to pay the loan on Buck's Indian elephants. I had been dropping in to see Mr. Spreckels occasionally, and one day I asked him why he didn't help us with our elephants.

"I will," he answered, "providing you can get whiter elephants than some I have now," and chuckled appreciatively at this reference to his unhappier business deals.

That was one joke that would boomerang on its maker, I determined! The next day I bought a large keg of white powder and four of the largest powder puffs I could find, went back to the Zoo and set the keepers to experimenting on the elephants. The result was eminently satisfactory. The next problem was to get Mr. Spreckels to the Zoo. I mapped out a little campaign and, over a period of some time, talked to him on every possible occasion about fights between king snakes and rattlesnakes until at last—to my great relief—he asked to see one.

Never had a snake fight dragged so maddeningly! An hour and a half crawled by before we could call the king snake victor and rush Mr. Spreckels over to the elephant compound where the men had been busy wielding valiant powder puffs. There stood the two snowy

John D. Spreckels (center) is about to give the "white" elephants to the Zoo in a dedication ceremony led by Rep. George Burnham (left). Dr. Wegeforth is on the right.

white, bulging beasts—looking like nothing any mortal had ever seen, their black eyes and pink mouths the only spots of color in the large white expanse. The keepers carried out the white color scheme, for they too were covered with powder from head to foot.

Mr. Spreckels laughed heartily at the fantastic picture and promised to pay not only for the loan but for the compound as well, and sure enough, in the first mail we received his check for $7,500. That night he gave a dinner at Hotel del Coronado, and I really believe he got his money back in his delight in telling the story. It made the hit of the evening.

Mr. Spreckels became a loyal admirer of the Zoo. Some time later, he and I, with the collusion of Queenie and Empress, staged a little political work for a friend, U. S. Senator Shortridge, a good old Republican who was running for office again. "Joy" and "Happy" had been chosen by the children of San Diego in popular vote as new names for their elephants, and Senator Shortridge rechristened them. Pictures of the ceremony were distributed all over California—pictures that showed the Republican nominee standing beside the emblem of his party. The elephants, however, repudiated their new names by refusing to answer to any but those they had brought with them, and so Queenie and Empress they remained.

■ ELEPHANTS CAUSE HEADACHES   93

Impressed with the weighty responsibility of owning two elephants, I read everything I could find about elephants and relayed all my newfound knowledge to Buck and the other keepers. Among other things I learned that the custom of oiling their hides had caused many deaths, for sometimes acute Bright's disease or pneumonia developed, especially when there was a change in temperature. Nevertheless, Buck oiled them and they quickly developed Bright's disease. They became very piteous-looking creatures, their trunks grew flaccid and seemed about a foot longer than usual, and their abdomens

The Zoo's elephants (c. 1920s) swimming in their new enclosure with local "bathing beauties."

almost touched the ground. I was afraid they were doomed. We mixed epsom salts with bran and, by using alfalfa meal, at last caused their bowels to move and relieved them of much of the edema. Some time passed before they were able to use their trunks, but eventually they were as well as ever.

When I returned from San Francisco a few months later to find Buck had oiled them again, although with less disastrous results than before, we terminated his employment. He sued us for breaking his contract and sued me personally as well, but after weeks of litigation, we won the case.

In 1926, we acquired our third elephant. Mr. Chris Holmes of Santa Barbara had on his ranch an elephant about six feet tall and a small pony that had formed a Jonathan-and-David attachment. One night Mr. Holmes was giving a polo banquet, and to crown the evening the pony was brought indoors in all his polo trappings to be admired by the guests. But the pony, little moved by all this glamor, neighed for his elephant comrade. The elephant began an anxious search, located his friend, and in trying to reach him became wedged in the doorway of the banquet room. So far as the Zoo was concerned, the result was a hurried call from Mr. Holmes telling us that we could have both pony and elephant if we would call for them. Culver, the elephant, was a very fine animal and we were delighted to get her.

Her entry into the elephant menage, however, created one of those notorious triangle situations. Empress promptly developed a "crush" on Culver, and if Queenie even came near her, Empress would flog her viciously with pile-driver blows from her trunk.

In time, Culver grew as large as the ponderous Empress herself, and wherever Culver was, trouble was sure to brew. Eventually, we wearied of being in constant hot water and sold her to a circus, where, I understand she showed no inclination to reform.

Queenie was a gentle and lovable elephant but Empress abused her like a chain-gang boss. Queenie had lost one eye, so we decided to sell her and get another elephant to companion Empress.

I became ambitious to breed elephants and began looking for a bull. In 1935, Barnes Brothers Circus wintered near El Monte, and as the manager had promised us some old canvas, Charlie Smith, our head animal man, and I went up. The manager showed us a fine though smallish bull named Prince with beautiful, strong tusks and offered to send him down to us. A chain clanked about his leg, for he was a killer. Nevertheless, I took him.

A female elephant chained to Prince escorted him down—a stodgy animal that could be counted on to keep him in line should he show signs of rebelliousness.

The beneficent climate of San Diego did nothing for Prince's moral regeneration. He continued vicious and only the keeper who fed him dared turn his back on him.

Specially constructed quarters were built for him, with electrically controlled gates, but it took almost a year after his arrival to complete them. When he was ushered into his new home, he walked straight over to the moat and tumbled down it. The moat was eight feet deep—not deep enough to hurt him but too deep for him to get out. Prince, usually such a bully, now shook with fright. We piled bales of hay in the moat until they were high enough for him to walk out. This is an old trick that circus men resort to when loading elephants on a car in a hurry, and Prince readily recognized what was expected of him.

Empress was to be his mate. She was led into the big pool enclosure and Prince, still with the chain on his leg, was also led out. He walked over to the water and stayed there at least two hours, rolling and tossing—enjoying himself in the water as I never saw another elephant do, but ignoring Empress as completely as though she were yet in the wilds of India.

At last he came out of the water but now he acted as though he had a stomachache. Empress kept shying away from him fearfully; she would come toward him holding her trunk up, and then back up again. After Prince lay down and then got up, he seemed to be in extreme pain and I was afraid he had twisted his intestine or had a colic attack. That

Queenie (left) was described by Dr. Wegeforth as "a gentle and lovable elephant." But her companion, Empress, "abused her like a chain-gang boss."

night he knelt down on his knees and his pain was so intense that we gave him a large hypodermic of morphine. The next morning poor Prince was dead.

Disposing of Prince's body was an arduous job. We cut him into pieces and sent him to the city dump to be burned with oil. It took about two weeks and took such a prodigious amount of oil that the next time we lost an elephant, we simply buried him on the Zoo grounds.

In 1937 Cole Brothers Circus gave us two female elephants. Tommy was a bully and a rogue as far as elephants were concerned but tolerant enough of humans. Baby Boo, the other, was a dangerous animal with homicidal views on humans, but we decided to take them both and hope we got one good elephant out of the deal.

Tommy and Baby Boo were devoted to each other, and, in fact, Baby Boo could live with no other elephant except Tommy. Our men were confident that Baby Boo would become less malignant, but one day I saw her strike out at Ralph Virden, our construction superintendent. I decided it wasn't worth the risk to keep an elephant that was neither good all the time nor bad all the time, so we had her put down.

Then we tried to put Empress and Tommy together. Domestic strife ensued immediately. Even when watched, they were always juggling their positions to boot the other down the moat. Empress lost no time in convincing Tommy that she was boss. She would beat her unmercifully with her trunk, the thuds sounding as though she was wielding a big club. Poor Tommy would scream with pain and seemed greatly fearful of Empress' beating. She was game, however, and was always starting a scrap with Empress, though she knew she would be the loser. We had to separate them. Finally, as the Los Angeles Zoo had no elephants, we gave her to them. There Tommy found peace and harmony at last; she was well-liked by her keepers and made an excellent exhibit for them.

When our new elephant enclosure was being planned, I arranged for the moat to be made ten feet wide. Then I went away on a trip, expecting the work to continue in my absence. On my return, I found the Board of Directors had halted it, for they thought the floor of the enclosure was too small. In allowing room to make the floor larger, the moat was cut down to eight feet. By that time I had forgotten just why I had specified ten. As soon as it was finished, I remembered: I had measured Empress' trunk-stretch and learned that it was 12 1/2 feet from her front knees to the tip of her trunk. The eight-foot width put the palm trees planted outside the moat nicely within her reach and she wasted no time in pulling them up and devouring the tops. To thwart her, I had spikes set around the edge of the enclosure. The spikes were not a success—a four-inch ledge stood out beyond the spikes providing just enough space for Empress to brace her front feet and gradually work her back feet up so she could stretch out and either still manage to reach the palms or lose her balance and go falling down into the moat. To make the spikes an effective barrier, it would have been necessary to put another row along the very edge of the moat.

The elephant barn under construction (background) with the hippo barn seen in front.

Before we could do anything about this, while I was away on another trip, Empress became frightened at a dynamite explosion and fell over into the moat, tearing her sides on the spikes. Then the men covered them with concrete, which of course made them worthless as a guard for the trees. We finally chained the elephants as the only solution.

When I travelled about Europe I found this elephant-tumbling-down-a-moat a fairly common occurrence. Most of the zoos had sharp spikes around the barriers and edges of the moat. However, except for one at Leipzig who fell down and broke her leg, I heard of no elephants injuring themselves. Mr. Heck of the Munich Zoo told me that an eight-foot fall for an elephant was comparable to a fall off a chair for a man and caused them great fright but little injury.

From Paper Plans to Reality

There was nothing haphazard about the development of the Zoo. Plans were worked out in detail, maturing only after a great deal of thought and study. We wanted individual areas for each group of animals. Knowing with what malevolent speed diseases can spread among animals, we wanted these areas some distance apart so that if an epidemic broke out among some of the animals, that area could be isolated and the Zoo would not have to be closed.

The layout of the Zoo grounds lent itself ideally to this end. I spent my leisure time riding my horse up and down the rabbit trails through the canyons and brush, studying the topography, selecting sites best suited for open grottoes and pools, deciding which animals would be best exhibited on the high level areas and which would stand the cooler

Official Guide ZOOLOGICAL GARDENS

San Diego Zoo map, 1925.

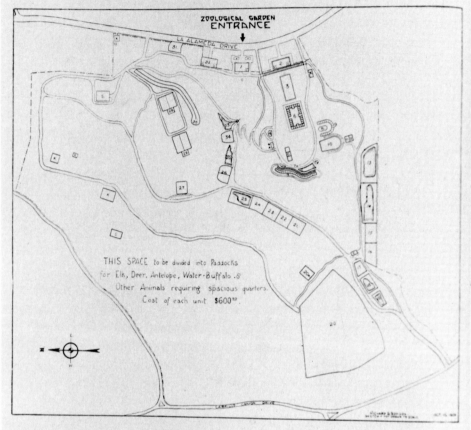

GUIDE MAP TO ZOOLOGICAL GARDEN

1. Entrance, Offices and Lunch Room
2. Reptile House
3. Seal Lagoon
4. Parrots
5. Apes
6. Monkey Group
7. Turtle Ponds and Burrowing Section.
8. Eagles and Hawks
9. California Small Birds
10. Flight Cage
11.–12. Storks
13. Goose Pond
14. Wild Duck Pond
15. Cassowaries
16. Emus
17. Peccaries
18.–19. Sea Birds
20. Bison and Elk
21.–22.–23.–24. Cranes, Herons, &c.
25. Sea Lions
26. Tigers and Cougars
27. Leopards
28. Camels
29. Elephants.
30. Pony Track
31. Bear Dens
32. O'Rourke Junior Zoo Building
33. Crocodile Pond
34. Lion Grotto
35. Alligator Pond
C. Comfort Stations
K. Keepers' Homes
S. Service Buildings

Above, Bum, an Andean condor, and his Keeper Karl Ring, c. 1930s. Left, Irish, a hooded or capuchin monkey, was given to the Zoo in 1927 by the crew of a fishing boat.

and less protected areas. The mesas (which were separated by canyons) were selected for the reptiles, birds, monkeys, the large animals and hoofed animals, and down in the canyons we put the bears and cats. The most expensive groups we placed on the side of a hill instead of a flat mesa; the combination of the sun and rains afforded a good likelihood that any infection in the cages would be eradicated each year, and the slanting hill diverted the rains so that they would not contaminate the next cages. Only the men were left as possible disease carriers, but as long as we needed keepers there was no way to eliminate that hazard!

The cost of maintaining the animals, the division of the work, and the number of keepers required to take care of the animals and grounds was worked out on cost sheets. Other zoos cooperated readily in giving us the menus they used, and thus we could arrive at a pretty accurate estimate of the cost of maintaining animals before we actually invested our money in them.

As for the animals themselves, we agreed to keep no single animal of any kind. I always felt—and other members of the Board felt likewise—that keeping a single animal in a zoo is like keeping a person in solitary confinement. Subsequently, on several occasions the accuracy of the comparison was strengthened when some of the primates showed distinct signs of dementia after living alone for a long period. Although they may have cousins close by, they seem to need a companion in their own cage.

In most cases we had to be content with a pair (which in Zoo parlance always means one male and one female) of the large and expensive animals, though best of all we liked to have a trio of one male and two females. Sometimes certain animals are very difficult to procure, and, with this combination, if we lost one female we still had a chance to increase our exhibit by the phenomenon of birth. Also, one cannot always tell the age of an animal on purchase; animals in fine hair and good physical condition, if adult, in a few years may become senile and not much of a show. Our trio arrangement made it likely that we could replace the decrepit ones. A third advantage of such a trio was that with two breeding females, there are good possibilities of having a pair of young to dispose of, and, of course, a pair finds a much quicker market than a single specimen.

It was never the Zoo's purpose to have a large number of any one species of animals. A fair collection of the outstanding animals was to be kept, and as the Zoo became more financially robust, we were to replace the most common animals with more select rare specimens. In short, we were going to make ours a Zoological Garden with a notable group of animals that could be seen in but few zoos and let ordinary zoos display the common varieties. This has been our policy through the years.

Miss Ellen Scripps, one of our most generous donors, used to visit the Zoo two or three times a week until illness compelled her to remain at home. She evinced a lively interest in our progress, questioning me about our plans, and was always eager to know what our next exhibit would be.

One day in 1922, Miss Scripps came into my office and said she had been pondering over the Zoo and felt that what we needed was a full-time man with some knowledge of animals who could also help me with the building program and shoulder much of my work and worry. Frank Stephens had been acting as Director but he was able to devote only part of his time to the Zoo and received no salary. She concluded by volunteering to pay the salary of such a man for three years. I remarked that a man equipped to assume such a job would command about $5,000 a year, and she replied, "Well, see if you can find someone and I'll take care of that."

I recollected hearing of a young university graduate employed in the Boston Zoo who had majored in zoology and had also worked as a keeper in the New York Zoological Gardens until he had gained broad practical experience. The Boston Zoo had planned ambitiously to put two million dollars into a zoological garden, but when the administration changed, this rosy project melted away like a mirage in the desert. Hence this young man was looking for more fertile pastures for his talents.

His reply to my wire came quickly—he was definitely agreeable to the proposition. I boarded an eastbound train to interview him, but when I got off at the other end, he had accepted a position with the Chicago Zoo at $6,500. Several years later he told me he had always regretted declining my offer, for the building of the Chicago Zoo had been postponed four or five years and his own position became more a matter of salary and glory than of actual work—a grievance he would never have had with us.

Disappointed, I decided to go on to New York to see if Dr. Hornaday, director of the Zoo there, could tip me off to a promising young director. A less obstinate man than myself would have been disheartened by the repeated rebuffs I met on this trip; not only did Hornaday refuse to assist me with my director problem, but he also tried to discourage me about the whole project of a San Diego Zoo. Why he took this attitude, I never learned. Later, when he visited San Diego, he came to the Zoo, walked as far as the monkey houses—and would go no farther.

Perhaps after my departure he regretted his abruptness. Anyhow, to my great surprise, Frank J. Buck called me in San Diego saying he had been referred by Dr. Hornaday. Buck was on his way to India to "bring back alive" a shipment of animals, and we struck an agreement for him to collect some animals for us and to become Director of the San Diego Zoo when he returned. Buck came to work for us about June 1923.

As soon as we corralled half a dozen $300-to-$500 donations from sundry San Diego merchants for monkey cages, we began work on them. The contractor quoted us a price of $6,500. We presented his bid to the Board of Directors, but one member insisted that we adopt a plan by which the contractor would receive an amount equal to 10 percent of the cost of labor and material, assuring us we would save money this way. To our dismay,

A drawing of the proposed lion grotto, "without iron bars protecting the public," appeared in a local newspaper.

work was completed we found ourselves indebted for $14,000, or more than twice the original bid. This was an extortionate price to pay but it seared our lesson into us. Never again did we enter into a contract in which we were not protected by a limit.

At every opportunity, I visited eastern and northern zoos until I had seen practically every important zoo in the country. However, none of these would serve as a pattern for us; their animals had to be sheltered from summer rains and winter cold, while we felt we needed to provide nothing more than sleeping quarters and shelter from infrequent showers. Therefore, we reversed the plans used in the east; there animals are usually exhibited indoors in cages along the walls, and here we made the cages part of the outside wall and constructed sleeping quarters and a service yard behind them where the men could perform their duties.

This scheme was carried out especially in the reptile house, parrot, pigeon, and monkey cages. It has proved highly satisfactory for many reasons: first, the men have ample space in which to work in private; second, being outdoors, the fresh breezes blow the odors away; third, if an animal escapes, he escapes merely into the service yard, which is wired over, and is very soon recaptured; fourth, if the animals weary of being in the public eye, they can retire to solitude in their sleeping quarters.

Although most of our donations were secured through the laborious process of going to citizens and getting them interested enough to contribute, occasionally an unexpected sum came to us like manna from heaven. Such was the origin of the pool that now accommodates the penguins. When we excavated for the monkey cages, space was left for the pool but we had no funds to construct it.

After the cages were completed, we held a dedication ceremony, and I overheard a woman scolding one of the keepers because she could see no private shelter for monkeys. I took her back of the cages where the monkeys had ample sleeping quarters. When we came out she wanted to know why the monkey cages were so far from the reptile house, and when I told her of the contemplated pool, she wanted to know why we did not build it immediately. "No funds," I answered drily. She replied that we should go ahead with it and she would foot the bill. In August 1922, the Mirror Pool was completed. First the swans lived in it, then the elephant seals, and, finally, penguins.

Next, we tackled the lion grotto. This time the wolf was not nipping at our heels and we did not have to resort to floor-eliminating devices. The grotto was to be designed like a pit, and as I knew of none similar in this country, we had to work out every detail of our virgin plan. A Hollywood film company made tests for us to ascertain how deep we needed the pit—tied a lump of meat on a rope, and raised it higher and higher to see how high the lions would jump.

We selected the floor of the canyon for the location. The Park Department temporarily punctured our plan by refusing to let us build a road down to the grotto. The problem of getting the material down was a formidable one. We finally solved that by laying a little track back of the elephant pen and carrying it down to the grotto. All material had to go down on this track in a small truck worked by cable. Concrete was constructed into blocks, each with an opening in the center, and sent down to the canyon where they were strung on reinforced iron bars. This sent the cost of the grotto soaring well beyond what we had estimated. We used streetcar rails for the framework—just as is done with great steel buildings—and the blocks were set in between reinforcements.

When the men began finishing the grottoes, I saw at once that we had erred in employing only first-class cement workers. Instead of irregular lines that would have a natural, undulating grace, all the lines were as painfully straight as if made with a ruler. We had them taken down and laid again with less scrupulous perfection.

The Park Department could hardly object to our hewing a pedestrian path down to the canyon, so we had Mike Kelly, our handy man, begin one next to the bear grotto and carry it down to the canyon. This was widened a few inches from time to time, and eventually we had good road. Today every road in the Zoo is wide enough for two trucks, except that in the lily dell.

Mike, incidentally, was a genius with a pick. He was the Zoo's sole construction man, except for those sent in by firms building under contract. Many an hour I used to sit and talk while he was resting, watching him demonstrate how he could strike a match with the end of his pick. I often think of Mike when I walk or drive down our fine broad roads, for they all evolved from paths constructed by him.

The completed lion grotto with its benefactor, Ellen Browning Scripps, in the foreground. Opposite, Prince the lion, one of the Zoo's first residents, in the new exhibit.

Not long after finishing the lion grotto, we built two large pools having for their retaining walls replicas of the Otay Dam built to scale. In these we placed sea lions that we planned to rear as commodities for exchange and sale.

Crusading for Antivenin

The love of animals (like other human loves) manifests itself in unpredictable ways. For instance, in San Diego when I first began to forage about for our Zoo, I encountered four or five families who had adopted wildcats as pets. Most of them landed up at the Zoo as donations in the end, for our local bobcat lacks the equanimity of mind to become docilely domesticated. Other cats that I would have expected to make far more mutinous pets—such as the ocelot—became affectionate and friendly to strangers when adopted as house animals.

Many wealthy persons, I found, had backyard zoos. Some of these were not merely half-a-dozen monkey affairs, but included bears, tigers, leopards, elephants, deer, and other large and costly animals. From time to time, too, surprisingly, people of moderate means would come in and give us presents of rare birds from their aviaries.

The snake, of course, exercises a traditional sinister fascination for people. But adopting poisonous snakes as pets is certainly succumbing too drastically to the fascination! I recollect one gentleman who showed me his pet red rattlesnake, a very large specimen that did not seem to mind him handling it. When I cautioned him to be careful, he laughed and said, "Oh, I've had him for years. He's very tame." Tame or not, a few weeks later I read an announcement of his funeral, the swift result of the snake's biting him. The rattlesnake can kill its victims in a shockingly short time. Roscoe Hazard told me of a farmhand on his ranch in Arizona who jumped across a ditch; as he fell on his hands on the other side, a snake struck him in the neck. Men who were nearby saw him walk nine steps and then fall down—dead.

In 1922, a small girl and two boys were struck by rattlesnakes in Balboa Park. This served to make me sharply snake-conscious. I learned that a local pharmacy was selling to credulous purchasers a case containing a tourniquet and a so-called antivenin that was nothing more than a solution of permanganate and caffeine. We exposed this fraud through the newspapers and embarked on an effective crusade to educate San Diegans about snakebite and antitoxin.

At that time antitoxin had to be brought from the Pasteur Institute in Paris. In San Diego, it simply was not available. We decided to pioneer the field and the Zoo began to import the serum. No halfway measures for us—we even arranged to rush it to outlying districts by plane, for it was guaranteed as a cure only if administered within four hours after the bite. In one instance, we delivered the serum by plane to the back country near

Escondido where a child had been struck by a rattlesnake, thirty-five minutes after the phone message had been delivered. We did not charge for the serum, only for the airplane trip. There was a pleasing touch of the dramatic about this act of mercy—the plane would fly to the vicinity where the stricken victim awaited and a parachute containing the emergency kit with instructions was released and lowered to the ground. The *San Diego Union* of May 15, 1922, gave us a colorful spread, featuring a photo of an airplane hovering above a rustic scene, with the parachute suspended just before it fell.

I remember a lion tamer who applied to us for work. As there was a prospect of something opening up in about a week, he remained in town. One day he went to Point Loma, where he saw a rattlesnake. He picked it up, thinking it would be a welcome tenant in the Zoo. He had handled many snakes and knew all about grabbing them back of the head. "But," he complained to me, "this one had an India-rubber neck." It twisted and bit him on the thumb.

I read of his accident in the papers and called the hospital. "Doing nicely," they told me in glib hospital vernacular, adding that he had been given antivenin. Three days later a friend of his telephoned me in distress, saying that he had not slept since the bite, his arm was black to the shoulder, and he was actually dying. I visited him and found him in very bad shape, perspiration beads clustered on his forehead, and his pulse galloping. The only treatment he had had was an injection of permanganate of potash. We gave him a hypodermic of antitoxin, and in a couple of hours his pain began to ease up and he fell asleep. He recovered shortly thereafter.

Even the contractors whose mules were struck by rattlesnakes began to come in for the antitoxin. Snakebite did not seem to be fatal to mules but crippled them badly and sometimes left open sores. When treated with antivenin, they were able to return to work much sooner than if treated otherwise.

Why a great scientific nation like ours should have to send across the seas to Paris for antivenin was too profound for me to grasp. In fact, in common with many others, I could see no reason at all. Dr. Raymond Ditmars of the New York Zoological Society, along with our Zoo in the West, began an intensive publicity campaign on snakes and snakebite. We compiled statistics by writing to each state in the Union, proving that about two hundred deaths are caused yearly by rattlesnake bites. This publicity, I believe, was instrumental in inducing Mulford & Company of Philadelphia to manufacture an antitoxin specific against rattlesnakes. They engaged Dr. de Amaral of the famous Butantan Snake Farm in Brazil where antivenin had been produced for many years. Nor did the Zoo play a negligible part in this venture—Mr. Klauber milked our rattlesnakes once a week for their venom, dried it, and sent it on to Mulford's, where it was injected into mules and the antitoxin was eventually produced.

At first the Zoo was the only place in San Diego that stocked antivenin, but, before long, most of the drugstores and hospitals in the city kept a supply on hand. San Diego was the first in the use of antivenin, and we are proud of our leading role in familiarizing the people with its use and the consequent saving of lives.

Later, a suction cup was designed that proved very successful in treating the poison and, to a large degree, supplanted antivenin.

We Buck the Animal Dealers

When in 1922 we began to look around speculatively with an eye to enlarging our animal collection, we were abruptly brought up against the animal dealers. In the role of middlemen, they would buy animals from one zoo and sell them to another—often in a neighboring city—at a great hike in price. Too, they would sometimes corner the market of available stock and send the price skyrocketing. In looking for kangaroos, I found that a certain New York dealer, with true Wall-Street aplomb, had cornered all the surplus kangaroos in United States zoos and also imported some from Australia, and had advanced the price from $300 a pair to $1,200. So the would-be kangaroo owner either bought $1,200 kangaroos or no kangaroos at all.

It seemed preposterous to me that a group of intelligent zoo directors could not get together and work out a plan whereby they would all know what surplus stock each had available. This thought blossomed in my mind: to have them contact foreign zoos for their mutual benefit, relative to importing such animals as they wanted. And that led me logically to the hope that a number of zoos would collaborate on expeditions, prorating the animals among them.

Paper plans radiate a beautiful simplicity but have a disposition to develop alarming complications when put into practice. My cooperative-zoo-action was no exception. I suppose I visited every zoo in the United States that had more than a peanut rating for support. Two private zoo owners who had built up admirable collections consented to join the organization and to assist in inaugurating it. One of them was Victor Evans of Washington, D. C., who then owned most of the animals in the National Zoo. The other was Percy Godwin of Nashville, Tennessee. They came to San Diego to meet with the members of the San Diego Zoological Society. Four men from St. Louis also arrived for this first meeting: George P. Vierheller, Fred W. Pape, Frank Schwartz, and A. D. Luehrman. A number of other zoos had signified their willingness to participate in the organization.

We decided to call ourselves the National Association of Zoo Executives, to organize as an auxiliary of the American Institute of Park Executives, and to include our contributions in their publication, *Parks and Recreation.* Later we met with the Park Executives Association in Washington, D. C., and Mr. Brown, director of the Philadelphia Zoo, accepted the chairmanship in order that we might interest more Eastern zoos.

Soon our membership list grew to 135. Then we began to receive requests from aquariums that they be allowed to join. We consented and rechristened ourselves the American Association of Zoological Parks and Aquariums.

The society flourished and in time became international. In addition to saving affiliated zoos tidy sums by eliminating the middlemen, the discussions and exchange of experiences proved of inestimable value.

We Turn Seal Hunters

Our first elephant seal was brought from Guadalupe Island by Mr. Ernest Dort on one of the U.S. Naval Reserve boats, after we had obtained a permit from Mexico for its capture.

Proud of our seal, we took the swans out of the Mirror Pool and set the seal in this place of honor. Not long afterwards, Professor J. N. Gallegos, an official of the Mexican Government, insisted that the seal be turned over to him, claiming our permit was not from the proper authorities, although it had been issued by the Governor's Office in Lower California. To avoid controversy and with the consent of Mr. Dort, we sadly donated our seal to the zoo in Mexico City. Since then the Mexican Government has always been very ready to let us have what seals we required. Professor Gallegos became a good friend of ours, and through him many prominent citizens of Mexico City have become very pro-San Diego Zoo.

The following year, the U.S. Naval Reserves sent an old submarine chaser back to Guadalupe Island; this time, before leaving they were armed with a permit to capture seals. The *Koka*, a Navy tugboat—with myself aboard—followed close after them, skeptical of the submarine chaser's ability to make the trip alone, particularly with its amateur crew. We captured four, handsome seals; two of them died before we got them to the pool. This trip taught us to keep water running constantly on the seals to assure getting them to San Diego alive.

On either side at the lower end of Mirror Pool we placed ramps to allow the seals easier passage out. They have little stored energy, tire very quickly, and it is quite an ordeal for them to lift themselves over a ledge. Later, the advent of the penguins ousted the seals from Mirror Pool and we transferred them to a pool in one of the canyons.

In April 1922, a seal was washed up on the sand at Ocean Beach and was brought to the Zoo. Several scientists in the city examined him and declared him to be a fur seal, for under his hair he had a fine coat of fur. The newspapers gave us generous publicity on our sensational find. Later, to our mortification, we learned that some of the California hair seals have fur under their hair, and from then on we were humbly silent about our fur seal.

This incident kindled my interest in the fur seal. I besieged every fisherman I met with

Marie the walrus, a favorite "salt-water character" at the Zoo. Below, seal collection during the early 1930s.

Dr. Charles Townsend of the Bronx Zoo with Galápagos tortoises brought to the San Diego Zoo.

inquiries, as well as anyone who had ever visited the islands along the coast of California and Lower California. I learned that years ago hundreds of thousands of fur seal skins had been sent to Russia and Europe from these islands, but the animal was now supposed to be extinct. I resolved to try to locate the remnants of those once vast herds.

One day a fairly well-educated man came into my office, his arm badly infected from a fishhook wound. He owned a fishing boat on which he and his wife lived and comprised the crew. This man described a seal he had seen on his trips, which he thought was a fur seal. What exciting news! I told him that if he would capture two of them for us, we would bear the expenses of his trip. After six or eight weeks, his arm well again, he sailed, returning with two fur seals. He said he had seen hundreds of these on Guadalupe Island, where they were once killed in great numbers. We paid him $750 for the two seals, based on his time and the expense of the trip. These were the first Guadalupe fur seals ever seen alive in the United States.

Dr. Charles Townsend dropped in on us the day after their arrival, bringing some Galápagos tortoises that he wanted to keep at the Zoo for experimental purposes. It was Dr. Townsend who had originally classified these seals from the skulls that were found on Guadalupe Island, and they had become known as *Arctocephalus townsendii*, or Townsend fur seals. These were the first of his namesake seals that Dr. Townsend or any other scientist had ever seen alive.

The two seals were kept at our Zoo for an exceptionally long time. When they died, they were skinned; one skeleton and tanned hide were sent to the Mexico City Museum, and the other to the American Museum of Natural History in New York, where it is still on exhibition, prominently placed in the Marine Mammal Hall. It was only after the skeleton reached New York that the seals were unmistakably identified and officially recognized as the "lost fur seal."

My bargain with the fisherman included his describing the location where he had found the seals. He did so but must have misinformed us, for although we made many trips to the island, we never did find them. It was as though that herd, too, had slid into extinction.

Still standing, however, were the rock walls of the dwellings in which Aleutian islanders, brought to Guadalupe by Russian sealers, had lived. Stakes used in drying the skins remained on the southern slopes of the once-populated seal rookery. Although Guadalupe Island is a cold, bleak place, very little rain falls, and such things will remain there for years unless destroyed by humans. The rocks along the beach were worn smooth and shiny from seals crawling over them during the many centuries that they used it for their rookery.

At first our seals (as the California sea lion is commonly called) were derived from two very variable sources. Every once in a while a zoo-minded fisherman would call on us and present us with a seal he had brought up from southern waters. Occasionally, too, we augmented our collection by capturing some of the imprudent seals that flopped up on the beaches near San Diego for relaxation. Since we were close to a teeming supply, we decided to launch into the sale of seals to zoos and circuses and thus relieve our chronic financial cramps. We now needed seals in much larger quantities and entered into a blanket agreement with a number of fishermen who were to use specially made nets to capture them.

Although the device of continuously running water on the seals brought up from the islands usually insured that they arrived in the harbor alive, once there they frequently grew so excited over the extraordinary turn their lives had taken that they would become overheated and die before reaching the Zoo. Later we learned that if they were cooled off sufficiently just before leaving the docks, a quick trip to the Zoo could be effected without injury to them.

Sometimes the seals refused to eat when brought to the Zoo, and we had to wait until they came off their hunger strike and became healthy, plump specimens before they could be sold.

Transporting them to other zoos and circuses brought its own convoy of trouble. They frequently died crossing the desert, and even the sun beating down on them for a few minutes was often fatal. A famous curator of an Eastern zoo once told me they had seven seals arrive in excellent condition, and all seven of them died within a few minutes when one of the men left them in the sun beside the pool while he went to lunch. If this new venture of selling seals was to fatten our budget, I would have to think of some way to get them through alive.

One day I noticed that ice wrapped in gunny sacks melted very slowly. Why not try this on top of the crates? Why wouldn't the constant drip of cold water keep the seals cool? We experimented and it proved to be our solution. The ice would last from one inspection point of the American Railway Express to the next, where it would be replenished. From that time on, we lost no seals en route, although we have shipped hundreds all over the world.

The Zoo's first seal trainer, Captain Charles Vensen, presented his first show in 1928.

In 1928 we employed a keeper who was also a seal trainer and have never been without one since. Now, six days a week we have trained seal performances. Many of our trained seals have appeared in moving pictures. The traffic in seals and our revenue from their movie appearances have combined to make the seal our most lucrative animal, and we owe it a debt of gratitude for its part in having made possible our fine animal collection as well as some of our structures.

The Director Problem is Solved

As 1922 drew to a close, the Harvester Building was turned into a combination reptile house and Zoo entrance. An aisle ran from the front to the rear of the building. On each side of the aisle, a large, oblong, concrete pool was built; one of these housed lizards, tortoises and the like, and the other provided a home for water snakes.

In the center of the latter, stumps had been placed where the snakes could climb and preen themselves. Stones set in concrete were heaped about the edge of the pools; there was no way of heating the building and these stones gave it a somewhat clammy and cheerless appearance. We soon replaced them with flower boxes, and these made it more cheerful if not warmer. Reptile cages about 4x4x4 feet, opening from the top and planted with small trees, ranged in rows. Quarter-inch mesh wire was used for the front of the cages, for glass was beyond our means at this stage. The wire was painted black, and as long as it didn't become too dusty, the visibility was good. Poisonous snakes had a double screen so that experimental visitors putting their hands on the screen would not be struck.

Our staff was very small. Mrs. Maud Scott acted as doorkeeper and information clerk, with various members of the Board of Directors relieving her for lunch.

We advertised for an experienced reptile man and were deluged with self-styled reptile experts. Sometime, somewhere, they had all caught snakes and seemed to think that put the stamp of specialist on them. We had to be satisfied with getting someone who could catch snakes and knew enough to keep out of the rattler's way.

The problem of properly naming the snakes then confronted us. There was one man in the city, I knew, who if once interested, would be able to supply the scientific names as well as the common names and would be a spark plug for that department. That man was L. M. Klauber of the San Diego Gas and Electric Company. I talked to him at length several times and found him eagerly responsive. Later he joined our Executive Committee, and our collection of snakes and our scientific work on reptiles are in large part traceable to Mr. Klauber.

Our first really large collection of snakes—both rattlesnakes and harmless—was gleaned from the Zoo grounds itself. During the building of the dams, each day the workmen brought up a contingent of snakes. We put up fences and started our collection. Thus we actually "produced" snakes as well as exhibited them! I wonder if there is another zoo where the staff collected specimens from their own grounds and even used them to trade to other zoos.

It was well that we had such an abundant supply of snakes, for besides giving us something to exchange with other zoos, our unheated quarters caused many casualties and constant replacements were necessary. By a happy (for us) circumstance, we acquired heating equipment for the reptile house: the local firemen gave their annual dance in one of the park buildings, the furnace became overheated, the building burned down, and the firemen, instead of indulging in fun and frolic, spent the night fighting the fire. I had come out to watch the excitement, and after the debris was cleared away I found the heating equipment practically intact. We managed to get this donated to us, excavated for a cellar under our reptile house, and installed our first heating plant. This made a little more livable domicile for our reptiles out of the building that had never been intended for a reptile house in the first place.

It became increasingly evident that we would have to tap some more regular source of income to supplement our fluctuating donations, if our staff were to be developed. We decided to charge an admission fee. A survey of the Zoo grounds was made the first day of September, 1922, and about 12,500 linear feet of wire fencing put up. Miss Ellen Scripps bore the cost, and on January 1, 1923, we instituted a 10-cent fee for adults, with children free. However, the 10-cent fee netted us little more than a drop in the bucket of our growing expenses. Finally, in 1927, we raised it to 25 cents, continuing to admit children under sixteen free.

Frank Buck's shipment from India had included a 23-foot, 200-pound python, Diablo by name, who would not do his own eating and had to be force-fed. At first we had large sausages made of mixtures of horse meat, fowl, and rabbits which we forced down his throat. It took six men to hold him and a tub full of meat mixture to feed him. Afterwards, we put him in a box and kept him there for several days.

An article appeared in the paper describing the force-feeding and so many people were curious to watch it that we gave a public exhibition at the Zoo. So many more people attended this that we saved the stunt for a device to raise money when the Zoo was hard pressed by creditors. All during this snake's life, it never once ate of its own volition, yet it lived longer and more healthily than snakes who ate normally. And this in spite of the fact that the only heat it had was in its box and that was just from electric light globes.

We were looking for improved methods of force-feeding our python, and the second we tried was covering a bamboo pole with meat, thrusting this down his throat, sliding the pole out and leaving the meat in. Then one day I happened to be in a packing house, watching the preparation of sausage. "Why not?" I murmured. Back at the reptile house,

THE DIRECTOR PROBLEM IS SOLVED

we took a large sausage stuffer, put a six-foot length of small hose on it, passed the hose down the snake's stomach and ground the meat into it. Later we mixed bone, cod-liver oil, and other items of the snake's diet in with the meat. The sausage-stuffer method answered our force-feeding problem admirably.

As related elsewhere, Frank Buck's employment with us terminated in September 1923. Buck was followed by T. N. Faulconer, who had been executive secretary of the Board of Park Commissioners. Richard A. Addison came next. Poor Addison was subject to extreme seasickness—even the calmest water induced an attack. We sent him to the Gulf of California for birds, and he became so violently ill he had to be sent to a hospital for several days.

In October 1925, we applied to the Civil Service for a substitute to relieve our bookkeeper, who had taken a two-week vacation. Thus Belle J. Benchley walked into the Zoo's life. Though she had little business training, at the end of the two weeks she had proved herself highly competent, always carrying out my instructions to the letter. I decided to keep her. Joe Brennan called up, wanting her to work for the Harbor Department, but I persuaded him to leave her here.

From then on, I unloaded onto Mrs. Benchley's capable shoulders many of my onerous duties. One of the tasks I was most grateful to be relieved of was speaking at luncheon clubs. Chicken was "the thing" for luncheons just then, and if all the chicken I had consumed that year were laid end to end, I am sure it would have reached clear to San Luis Obispo. At first, Mrs. Benchley heartily disliked public speaking, and each appearance was preceded by an acute attack of nervousness. Before long, however, she was doing this with the admirable efficiency that characterized all her work.

I had been personally handling the trading and selling of animals, but before long, with a vast sigh of relief, I turned this, too, over to her.

In the latter part of 1926, Robert Bean, son of Ed Bean, director of the Milwaukee Zoo and one of the best zoo men in the country, came to work for us. Young Robert had majored in zoology and his work under his father at the Milwaukee Zoo had given him an excellent practical background. Shortly after Robert's arrival, we sent him to Australia for animals; he had just been married and his wife went along, transforming this into their honeymoon. After some time, he left us to accept a position as assistant to his father at the Brookfield Zoological Garden, Chicago.

None of the relationships with the men were entirely satisfactory. Either I did not get along with them or the Board had some objection to them. Finally, the Board said there would be no more directors or superintendents, that it was impossible to build a Zoo under two different theories, and that we would simply employ a secretary as assistant to myself. Then I could train someone upon whom I could rely.

Mrs. Belle Benchley came to the Zoo as a substitute bookkeeper in 1925, and would remain until 1953, when she retired as the Zoo's director.

More and more I had begun to see that in the able Mrs. Benchley lay the solution to our executive problem. I outlined my plans for her advancement to the Board. So far as we knew, no woman had ever filled a position of such importance in a zoo, and the Board felt it would be an experiment with an element of risk. They reiterated that there would be no more superintendents or directors—that we would organize a zoo staff similar to the one in London, with an executive secretary who would work under the Board of Directors.

In time, Mrs. Benchley became executive secretary of the Zoological Society. After four unhappy experiences with directors, the entire Board gave thanks that we now had someone who could be depended on. During the years that followed, my work at the Zoo, as a consequence, was a very pleasant task, and I no longer felt like Atlas carrying the Zoo on his shoulders.

Probably every zoo under the sun has had its quota of protestants who think it inhuman to keep animals in cages. Coupled with the many other sincere but troublesome persons who for some reason or other conclude that certain animals are being mistreated, they constitute a problem for zoodom.

Our Zoo arrived at a beautiful "out" by admitting three members of the Humane Society to the Zoological Society and routing all complaints to them. They inspected the animals once a week and made many helpful recommendations, which we followed out.

As soon as a vacancy occurred, Daniel Wray, president of the Humane Society, was made a member of our Board of Directors. Some criticism arose about Mr. Wray being on our Board while State President of the Humane Society. He resigned but continued to be a warm friend to the Zoo. Our relations with the Humane Society remained cordial, and we felt a kind of remote cousinship to them.

Now We're Land Owners

The School Board's request for six acres of land north of the Zoo grounds was placed on the ballot in 1922 and won by a good majority, for we all liked the idea of schools around the edge of the park. However, after the election it was discovered that the boundaries defined on the ballot had included a good deal of the Zoo grounds—and left us without passage from one mesa to another. The School Board had been unaware of this and when we entered our protest, they readily returned some of it to us. To compensate us for the portion of our land that they retained, the old Harvester Building (our present cafe) was given to us, and now our line extended down the canyon, running from the southwest corner of the building. Later on, the ground west of the Park Superintendent's cottage (the Model Farm of the Exposition) was turned over to us, along with a bottleneck that ran up to the present main entrance at the corner of Alameda and Calle de Colon, the fence extending down a canyon back of the Japanese Tea Garden and up to what is now our Research Hospital.

At this time Harry Warburton, Sam Fox, and Captain W. C. Crandall, all well-wishers of the Zoo, were on the Park Board and we were getting excellent cooperation on all our projects. However, we had some controversy about the fence line on the south border of the Zoo grounds, west of the Research Hospital. The superintendent and various members of the Board of Park Commissioners had conflicting ideas as to where our fence should go; even after the fencing was under way, the boundaries were changed two or three times until the map looked like sawteeth. Later, Lester Olmstead, a building contractor now on our Board of Directors, went on the Board and we were able to get a less angular profile.

My life as a Zoo official was colored by a parade of interesting contacts. Among those I enjoyed most were the animal importers and the hunters who captured animals in the wild. The postcards I occasionally got from them pungently brought the tantalizing aroma of far places into my office.

We could not have rated very high as customers, for most of our animals were obtained either through exchange or our own expeditions. Nevertheless, these men were generous with their advice and knowledge. The problem of transporting animals, for instance, is a very delicate one, complicated by the fact that usually the animals are on substitute diets. Undoubtedly, our Zoo was saved many a catastrophe by virtue of their advice.

From time to time we would run into curious people but none more curious than a young man whom Dr. Pickard of our Research Committee heard speak before the University Club. This fantastic young man claimed that, when five years of age, he had been wrecked and tossed up on the shore of eastern Africa with four other survivors. A band of chimpanzees, he continued fabulously, attacked and killed his companions but kidnapped him off into the jungle where he lived with them for many years, eating as they did and speaking with them. Then one day, so his story went, he fell asleep on the beach and awoke to find himself surrounded by a group of sailors. They took him aboard the ship and kept him there until they docked in Boston in 1919, when they turned him over to some scientists who taught him English.

Incredible as his narrative sounded, Dr. Pickard insisted it did have some of the ring of truth and brought him out to the Zoo. He and I, followed by a small crowd of people who had read about the young man in the local papers, walked with him down to the various monkey and ape cages to see if he could really "speak" their language. He climbed trees with the chimpanzees and they chattered back at him. Our keepers were startled, for they had never witnessed such behavior, even among the animals themselves. Young Tarzan next entered the baboon cage. Those vicious animals went up to him and chattered away as if he were one of them, although their keepers never dared go into the cages with them. Mike, the orang, wrestled with him good-naturedly, bit him playfully—and the strange young man bit back.

We asked him about his food in the jungle and he told us he had lived solely on meat, that he had caught rodents or whatever small animal came along, killed it and ate it. Dr. Pickard promptly presented him with a live guinea pig. He killed it, pulled the hair off with his teeth, and proceeded to eat it raw. Dr. Pickard and I remained grimly to see that he finished the job, but he seemed to relish it and never faltered. When he left us, we stood shaking our heads in bewilderment, still skeptical of his story but thoroughly convinced that he was a most remarkable young man.

Later we heard he had joined a show and hundreds of people came to watch him climb trees and live like his alleged former playmates.

Toward the end of 1922, the large flying cage for wading birds was begun. It measured ninety-six feet from its top to its lowest end and spanned across a canyon. We felt that dirt would be better for the floor than concrete, so only the two pools and the drain between them were concrete. The cage was dedicated on September 9, 1923, and within two months, the sloping dirt bank inside the cage was punctured with rat burrows. We hauled in slabs of concrete from broken-up paving and terraced the bank, filling in the crevices and covering the tops of the terraces with cement to repel the rats. Spots remained that were not thoroughly covered with concrete and, after several years, these broke through and rats again found a haven in the cage. Once again we filled up all the holes with concrete, and since then no rat has called this home.

Some eucalyptus trees were planted inside the cage to provide nesting places. These have pushed through the top several times and had to be trimmed. In the spring it is a moving experience to stand on the monkey mesa and look down into the cage—to see the birds on their nests, some sitting on their eggs, others feeding their young—the life history of the birds unfolding before your eyes.

In May 1923, Mrs. Patrick F. O'Rourke, who had become actively interested in our work with children, contributed the necessary funds to move the Standard Oil Building

Dedicated on September 9, 1923, the Scripps Flight Cage for shore and wading birds was eighty feet high. For scale, a man is seen standing on top of the structure.

across the street to the Zoo premises, where it could serve as headquarters for our Junior Zoological Society. After using the building for a short while, she concluded it was too small for lecture classes and told me to try to get the Nevada Building, another survivor of the Exposition that had been erected by the State of Nevada and was now owned by the Natural History Society. Mr. Harper of the Natural History Society's Board of Directors told us a wrecking company had already bought it.

When we reported to Mrs. O'Rourke, she said that if we could buy it from the wreckers, she would donate the money. We immediately contacted the owners and found the wreckers had an option on it and had paid only several hundred dollars. To abbreviate a long story, we finally managed to buy the option from the wreckers, who were very reluctant to sell it, by merely giving them what they had in it. Later, we persuaded them to donate the balance in the name of their children. I often think that the Exposition buildings we fell heir to were like a good, strong shot of red blood given a frail infant, for they spurted our growth immensely.

In looking over our book of newspaper clippings, I find a picture in the *San Diego Union* of November 11, 1923, showing the building ready for the foundation. This recalls to mind my consternation at seeing how high off the ground it was—for where was I to get the dirt to fill in under it? A providential coincidence furnished the solution: the city was beginning excavations for a large basement for the Fine Arts Gallery, and we bought 1,800 yards of the dirt. This gave us enough for our foundation and also helped to fill in a canyon that crossed the present road fronting the upper bear pit. As there was no retaining wall, the road caved in once or twice afterwards and had to be refilled, but none of the slides were serious.

These two buildings and the old Harvester Building were grouped into what later became known as the O'Rourke Buildings.

Of Camels, Chimp, and Snake

About the middle of 1923, word reached me that a Hollywood motion picture company that had imported camels for a picture was now looking for someone to sell them to.

There was no reason why our Zoo shouldn't have these camels! I knew that Shriners sometimes supply camels to their hometown zoos so they will be available for ceremonials, and I approached several members of the Al Bahr Temple. They invited me to attend their next meeting. There, assisted by some of the favorably disposed Shriners, I presented my request. It was so warmly received that I leaned back contentedly in my chair. Then one of the members, a lawyer who was averse to taking money from their treasury for whatever purpose, began to speak in opposition, exercising all his legalistic eloquence. I grew more and more alarmed as his fellow Shriners began to listen to him interestedly. It was a situation that called for prompt and drastic action—something to

Mrs. Frank Buck as she appeared in a San Diego Union article, June 24, 1923, with the Zoo's new camels.

arrest the spell of his rhetoric. Eureka, I had it!

Loudly and rhythmically, I began to chant, "We want camels, we want camels," pounding out the beat on the floor. Fortunately for my purpose, the innate love of music in man conditions him so he can never resist a chant. First, a few Shriners around me took up the words, and they quickly spread around the table until the speaker gave up in despair. They all had a good laugh and, in this mellow mood, voted the Zoo half the amount we had asked for the camels.

I went to Hollywood and purchased two camels for $1,500—and persuaded the film company to donate to us another female as a mate for Dick, the young male Bactrian camel Ringling's Circus had given us. The ones we purchased were dubbed Volstead and Bryan, for this was in the Prohibition Epoch. These four, with our two dromedaries (single-humped camels), Turk and Scar, gave us an excellent camel group.

We built a compound for the camels to represent as nearly as possible the roped enclosures we had seen in pictures—a simple arrangement consisting merely of posts set in concrete and ropes stretched around them. For posts we used steel rails covered with concrete, and an old elevator cable substituted for the ropes. In the spring, the camels' hair became loose and their heavy wool began to itch. They would rub themselves doggedly against the cables, and before long the compound was pretty well wrecked.

On July 28, the Shriners came up en masse and dedicated the camels to the children of San Diego, San Diego's Mayor rode splendidly in on the male camel, and Frank Frye, the Shriner's Potentate, less splendidly led the female, for he balked at riding her. Not long afterwards, the Shriners held ceremonials in one of the buildings in the park, and the camels, spread with oriental rugs, added their proud and impressive touch.

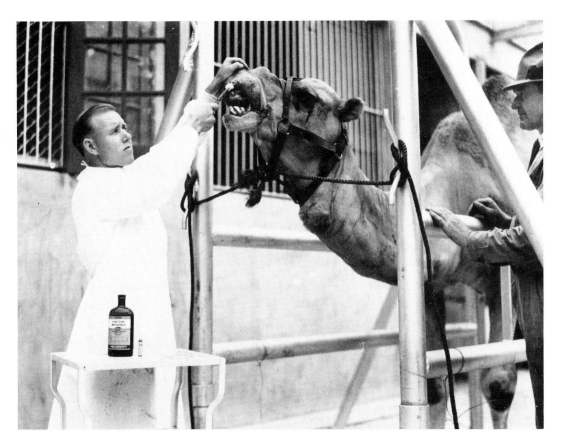

Dr. Charles Schroeder administering medical aid to Egypt, an early Zoo camel.

OF CAMELS, CHIMP, AND SNAKE

Our constant flow of Zoo stories in the papers—and obliging editors frequently featured them with compelling black lines—brought to us many interesting animals and some with notable pedigrees. Mr. and Mrs. Fred Weller left their huskies, descendant of Perry's North Pole dog teams, with us while they made a trip to Central and South America, where they thought it would be too hot for the dogs.

Then one day Snooky joined us. Snooky was a chimpanzee movie star in those days, better known—and much better loved—than many of the human stars. Mr. and Mrs. John Rounan had bought her from an animal dealer when she was a year old. They raised her on a bottle and treated her like a child. She reciprocated by acting like a very diligent one—helped them around the house, pruned the roses, mowed the lawn, ran the vacuum cleaner, and did numerous other little household chores. Some of these tricks, of course, were taught her to promote her movie career. When she came to us she was dressed in a shirt and tie and trousers. The Rounans parted from her dolefully, and it was a disconsolate Snooky they left behind.

They visited her frequently. Snooky would sense their presence five hundred yards away. She would rush frantically to the end of the cage nearest the driveway, yelling and calling to them, peering eagerly in their direction.

Snooky loved to ride in a car, loved to roller skate, but most of all she loved to smoke. She preferred cigarettes but was quite willing to compromise on a cigar or pipe. At first we were afraid she would set her quarters on fire, but she was more careful than a Boy Scout. After lighting her cigarette, she would shake the flame out and test it carefully with her finger to be sure it was out. When she finished the cigarette or cigar, she would drop it on the floor and meticulously mash out every lingering spark.

Snooky lived with us a long time, until the Rounans felt they could do without her no longer. Although she had been given to the Zoo, they were so happy at the prospect of being reunited that only a sadist could have stood between them.

Snooky met her end when a relative of the Rounans put her in a show at Long Beach one summer. There she contracted pneumonia and died.

In October 1923, I visited Dr. Ditmars, curator of reptiles of the New York Zoo. The night before, the glass in the India cobra pen had been cracked and Ditmars had tried to entice the snakes into an empty violin case. The plan failed because the opening had been made in the bottom of the pen and the cobra raises up when it is alarmed.

Reporters came in to get the story, and presently Walter Middleton of the Central Park Zoo also dropped in. As we sat chatting, Middleton began to tell us about an extremely rare pink, or albino, gopher snake his zoo had just been given. I perked up my ears, for in April of that year Mr. Klauber had left San Diego bearing with him for Dr. Ditmars a two-tailed lizard and a pink snake, gifts from our Zoo to the New York Zoo. In New York he had taken a room at the Commodore Hotel, and there both lizard and snake had escaped. The lizard was recovered behind a door, dead, but the pink snake was swallowed up in the vastness of New York, and that was the last Mr. Klauber saw of him.

I questioned Middleton about the origin of his snake, and he said it had been given to them by the management of the Plaza Hotel, which is located near Central Park. We went down in a body, reporters and all, to see the reptile. Beyond a doubt, there was our pink snake. The Central Park Zoo graciously turned him over to Dr. Ditmars.

The inexplicable tale of how the pink gopher snake got from the Commodore Hotel to the Plaza Hotel (some seventeen blocks distant) in the greatest metropolis in the world, consuming six months in the process, was featured in Sunday supplements in an article entitled, "The Mystery of the New York Zoo's Pink Snake."

The Mid-Twenties: A Roaring Time

Late in 1923, in my morning round about the Zoo, I noticed an outcropping of what looked like an old sea wall along the west edge of the monkey mesa. I hailed Mike, our handyman, and he walked over and began digging along the ledge to see what we would unearth. Colonel Milton MacRae, a friend of mine who was in the habit of visiting the Zoo periodically, dropped in just then and came down to watch our excavations. I pointed out to him several locations in the Zoo where prehistoric fossil whales were coming to the surface; one of those places was where the elk are now situated. He asked what plans we had for the ledge, and I told him I thought it a splendid place for owls and small hawks. He asked a few more questions and at length told me to go ahead and he would pay the cost. When the row of cages was finished, we wanted to put his name on it as donor but he insisted that we use the name of his grandson, John Paul Scripps. To us in the Zoo, however, these have always been known as the MacRae cages.

The path around these cages acquired a now-you-see-it-now-you-don't quality that was always a matter of concern. First, the dirt below the cages was spread out to form a path wide enough for people to walk on. The first good heavy rains that followed sent the path (in fact, the whole side of the hill, including a number of good-sized trees) sliding deep into the canyon. After that we gathered up all the rusty piles we could find, drove them into the ground, and packed the dirt on top.

This held for some time, but it was only in 1938 that a concrete wall supporting the walk was built and we could feel we had a path that would stay there. At the same time, shelters were built over the cages, and the stone construction of the cages that showed signs of erosion from wind and air was covered with concrete; however, even now some of the old blowholes and much of the sea wall remain intact and visible. Later, European sycamores were planted around the edge and the wall was then finished, with space below for an enclosure where someday we hope to station certain representatives of the stork family.

What few animals we had to exchange with other zoos we maneuvered to the best advantage. One of the first sources of income was lion cubs. During the first four years of our existence, we sold thirty cubs provided us by our obligingly prolific mother lions, at $150 apiece and up, according to their size and condition. One lion brought us $1,500, and a pair of half-grown cubs went to New York, netting us $800. Besides this, we traded seals. Then one lucky day, we discovered a rookery of white pelicans in the Salton Sea, which gave us a fine basis for exchanges for our aviary.

The year of 1924 was a banner one for the Zoo. This year our plans for the Research Hospital jelled and we began to talk importantly of its construction. The tiger grottoes, too, were finished this year. In 1924 came the birth of ZOONOOZ, our present monthly magazine. It was launched as a lively and provocative column in the *San Diego Sun*, filled with little stories of the Zoo and enlivened by some very good cartoons of our animals. W. B. France edited it.

In December 1924, we made our first really large shipment of animals. Full of pride, we sent off to Taronga Park, Sydney, Australia, a shipment of animals including alligators, rattlesnakes, monkeys, timber wolves, coyotes, desert lynx, and other small animals and reptiles. In return, we received two koalas, about forty kangaroos, some large birds, and other fauna of Australia.

One of the koalas arrived much the worse for the trip and died in a short time. The other lived with us for many years, setting a record for the length of time these delightful little animals had survived in captivity. Our enclosure for the koalas was built encircling a eucalyptus tree, for eucalyptus leaves are their chief item of diet. We had no way of knowing how old our koalas were and, hence, their life expectation. Small animals are often unknown quantities, for they may be full-grown when bought and, although in excellent condition, may soon become old and develop rheumatism and arthritis like their human brothers.

The koala is a nocturnal animal, not very active, and so would not be considered a desirable exhibit, except for the fact that their cunning and lovable appearance captivates almost every one who sees them. During the years our koala lived with us, he was one of our most popular attractions.

Another strange animal included in the Australian shipment was the echidna, one of nature's freak animals. The echidna lays eggs and then nurses its young after hatching them. Its beak is similar to a duck's and its body is covered with a sort of quill, like the porcupine's. It, too, was a nocturnal creature, and though we contrived for it to be kept in sight as much as we could, the keepers were the only ones who ever got a really good

Richard Addison, curator of mammals (1926), holds the Zoo's first two koalas, Cuddles and Snuggles.

look at it. During the day it rolled itself into a fur ball, and only when the sun was safely behind the horizon and dusk was deepening into darkness would it unroll and begin to prepare for its night life.

The auto camp next to the Zoo grounds—in fact, on what is now our deer mesa—was still extant in 1924. Appended was a grocery store and a poorly equipped comfort station. There was always a collection of broken-down autos parked around the camp. As each car emptied its passengers, they unfolded their tents and began housekeeping. The next thing they did was to wash their entire stock of clothing and spread it out on the grass to dry. You can imagine what an eyesore this was in the rustic loveliness of Balboa Park!

There were other disadvantages besides the scenic ones. Epidemics of burglaries frequently broke out. Furthermore, many of the transients carried dogs with them and it was not uncommon to see twelve or fourteen dogs tied up at the camp, barking ferociously, for some of them were obviously vicious.

Since the camp was contiguous to the Zoo, we determined to have it removed. This was a formidable task, for certain members of the Board of Park Commissioners were financially interested in keeping it there. We argued long and loud before the Board and the City Council, and with the able assistance of Fred A. Rhodes, City Manager and a Zoo fan, we eventually succeeded.

The closing of this camp led to the building of really adequate camps in various parts of the city. Before long, more than half a dozen camps with hygienic facilities were being constructed.

A proverb says that men are known by the enemies they make. The Zoo could claim renown on this basis, for we had our opponents as well as our friends. Some misled persons—as well as others who had their own political reasons—opposed having a Zoo in Balboa Park. A great deal of talk began to circulate about running a road through the Zoo grounds, not because the road was needed but because it would be a telling impediment to our growth.

About this same time, our yearly, harrowing difficulty in arranging our budget, together with the uncertainty of never knowing whether the animals we bought one year could be fed the next, led us to the decision to ask for a tax revenue—a two-cent tax on every hundred dollars' assessed valuation in the City of San Diego.

In the fall of 1925, therefore, voters found two amendments confronting them on the ballot: one that grounds be set aside for Zoo purposes, and the other covering the tax. Public interest rose to a high pitch. The Board of Park Commissioners, reluctant to lose jurisdiction over any of the park lands, opposed the first measure, and the President of the Board and myself—as President of the Zoological Society—debated the question one Sunday night at the Open Forum of the Unitarian Church. Much money was expended in the campaign against us, and day after day the newspaper-reading public would open its papers to find large, blazing ads warning them of how their interests would be jeopardized if they voted to support the Zoo. We, of course, had no money to flourish into paid advertising, but the papers again gave us liberal space on the front, as well as inside pages. With such respectable and monied forces aligned against us, we thought it a left-handed triumph that we lost only by a very small margin.

In 1926, Mr. and Mrs. O'Rourke withdrew from the Zoological Society and started a Junior Zoological Society under Mr. O'Rourke's name, using the Nevada Building for their headquarters.

Classes of schoolchildren chaperoned by their teachers had been coming to the Zoo in streetcars. I noticed that only about twenty children came in each class. Having read so much about the schools being overcrowded and understaffed, I inquired why the classes were not larger. The truth was that about a third of the people had no money for carfare.

It seemed more essential for these underprivileged children to come than those who

128   THE MID-TWENTIES: A ROARING TIME   ■

could afford it, for the latter could visit with their parents. Of course, the answer was bus service. The same lady who had built our Mirror Pool was interested in our educational work, and along in the middle of 1926 she donated enough money to buy two Model T Ford buses into which some thirty children could be sandwiched. (They also provided a source of income: when the schools were not using them, we transformed them into passenger buses making Zoo tours and charged a fee.) Our drivers spent the ensuing nights studying up on our animals and blossomed into creditable Zoo lecturers and instructors for the classes.

Alas, however, this happy arrangement became an easy victim when the depression set in. Then the streetcar company presented a proposition to the School Board to supply buses for the children, who would pay a reasonable fare. This was inaugurated but it did not prove profitable and was stopped in short order.

The general election of 1927 found the same propositions of 1925 on the ballot, divided into three amendments. This time we were able to effect a compromise with the Board of Park Commissioners and obtained their support for the tax and permanent granting of

The Zoo's first buses, used to tour the grounds, were an immediate success.

the grounds we wanted. In return, we agreed to withdraw our demands that the Zoo land be taken entirely from the jurisdiction of the Board of Park Commissioners. As the ballots had already been printed, we asked the people to vote against this part of the amendment. The voters made up their own minds, however—and voted for all three amendments.

But our opponents were not so easily bested by a mere people's vote! They quickly found a technical loophole: the law stated that all amendments must be published forty days before the election and ours had been published only thirty days before. This was indeed a blow. But now we were certain public sentiment was with us and settled down to a longer fight.

Into the Thirties: Fight Through to Security

About 10 o'clock one morning in 1927, just after finishing an operation, I dropped down to the Zoo Hospital, then in the old Standard Oil Building. Mrs. Benchley was standing on the steps and I joined her. The promise of rain hung heavily in the air. We looked to the northeast and saw black, thick clouds in the direction of Camp Kearney sending out a brisk sprinkling of rain. In the opposite direction equally dense clouds lowered, also dispatching a shower toward us. This phenomenon of two storms racing on the city was so absorbing that we stood, fascinated, watching them. They met just over what is now B Mesa (where the monkeys are) and, in the space of a few minutes, a cascade of rain—rivalling any tropical storm I have ever seen—was pouring down.

Soon water was flowing everywhere. Johnson, our foreman, came hurrying down to report that the canyons were beginning to fill with water. Braving the rain, we splashed down to F Canyon (the present home of the bears) and found some of the cages flooded. The tiger moat was brimming with water. Our Sumatran tiger had been swimming jauntily about but, as we reached her, she began to struggle to get out of the moat. Johnson lowered a ladder, climbed down into the moat, caught her in his arms, and pulled her out. I shuddered, for she was almost a full-grown tiger and I had often thought his friendliness with her did not leave a proper margin of safety. We closed the moats and locked the tigers up, for we were afraid there would be a cave-in. The road in front of the tiger grottoes was one mass of rushing water, and all around the mesa water was shooting down in falls—every two or three feet a strong stream spurted out as though someone had turned on a fire hose.

The storm lasted two or three hours. By the time it subsided, the water was waist deep in some of the canyons. We promptly started on repairs.

At that time, none of our men lived on the Zoo grounds. Alarmed at what might have been the story had the storm occurred at night, I jotted down the addresses of several of our men on a prescription pad and brought it home with me—never dreaming that within twenty-four hours we would have a repeat performance of the flood.

Shortly before midnight the rain began to drum down again. I rose and dressed, worried about the Zoo. On my way down, I stopped at 12th and C Streets where Johnson lived and brought him down with me. Just as we reached Laurel Street, a cyclone came hurtling through, uprooting eucalyptus trees and flinging them to one side. This diagonal swath of fallen trees extended from Sixth Street near Spruce to where the entrance of the park is today. In the Zoo, we found two eucalyptus trees twisted bare of all their branches that were lying just on the edge of what is now Fern Canyon.

By the meager illumination of our flashlights we could see the canyon was as flooded as it had been in the morning. The sea lions were swept out of the dam. Some of them were fighting helplessly against the force and speed of the water, which kept beating them back against the fences. We tore the fences down, hoping to divert the seals up on the hill, but they swam under the water and all seventeen of them went sliding down the canyon. In the morning several of them were found along 11th Street; some were found on the doorstep of the police station on 2nd Street, some in church entrances, and several were camped at the door of Marston's store. Two had taken refuge in garages and, when found, had hopped on top of the automobile. Several of them died from injuries incurred in their migration downtown.

This taught us that, in case of disaster, the Zoo could not afford to wait until men arrived from their homes. Soon afterward several dwellings were erected on the Zoo grounds, and now four or five families live in the Zoo.

In the 1929 election we omitted the amendment concerning the Zoo grounds and had only the 2-cent tax on the ballot, for on this there was no opposition. It passed by a comfortable majority.

It seemed as though we had to win our victories at least four times before they were ours. In August of 1929, local politicians decided that we needed a city manager form of government. When the plans for this were drawn up, our 2-cent tax was omitted but we were given unctuous assurances that not only did they favor the tax, but they also felt that we should get more money while we were building up the Zoo. Their after-the-election attitude reversed sharply, and we realized we had a real battle on our hands. Well, so be it. We marshalled our forces and sent innumerable representations to the City Council. Results were nil.

By 1934, we were convinced that we were getting nowhere fast and, for the second time, decided to appeal to the voters. Our brave little ZOONOOZ, proved of great help in getting our side of the story to the people. Mrs. Benchley covered meeting after meeting—a total of 206—with others covering what she couldn't. We rented headquarters downtown on B Street and set cages of monkeys and other small animals out-

TUESDAY, AUGUST 11, 1925

Our Motto: "The Same Backward, Forward or Upside Down"

ZOONOOZ

Published Every Now and Then

W. B. France Editor-in-Chief

Price, 5 minutes.

Balboa Park, San Diego.

Grand Midsummer Pictorial Number

Zoonooz takes pleasure in presenting its first grand midsummer pictorial number—the first and only thing of its kind ever attempted. If this unique undertaking meets with a favorable reception, it may be established as a regular sesquicentennial feature.

ENGAGEMENT RUMORED

—Photo by Averett

"We are merely encaged—but not engaged." With this statement both Alaska J. Huskie and Miss Cordelia Cougar denied high society gossip that Cupid had been busy with this popular twain. "He's a good musher, and I admire him as a gentleman friend, but he growls too much for a life companion," Miss Cougar declared.

"She's a nice girl, even if she is a little catty," Mr. Huskie confessed, "but she's too wild for me!"

✧ ✧ ✧

OF COURSE THEY DO!

"Of course movie actors use paint," Rudolph Valentino Bear, Zooville's famous film comedian, confessed to a Zoonooz reporter.

"Make-up is a necessary adjunct to cinema art, and a bit of paint here and there doesn't hurt anybody."

Rudy said later that his statement was confined exclusively to grease paint and drug store complexionery, —Photo by Fitch and that he condemned the use of so-called "wet paint."

✧ ✧ ✧

FUTURE CHAMP?

—Photo by Hartsook

Exclusive photo of L. A. Phant, heavyweight titleholder of Zooville, in training for his next bout. It is rumored that he will challenge Dempsey if he can raise the necessary $1,000,000 guaranty.

"Dempsey may be faster on his feet," the Zooville zoomer declared, "but I beat him on weight, and if I land a punch he'll never smell the flowers."

STUDIES ENGLISH

—Photo by Sensor

Tequila Concarne Peccary, who recently arrived from Mexico, is snapped by the alert cameraman while taking his lessons in English. His instructress is Miss G. G. Little of Harbor, popularly known as "Little Gee Gee."

"Tequila is a knock-out," she declared. "He is so quick he nearly takes me off my feet!"

✧ ✧ ✧

NOCTURNE

—Photo by Shimotsusa

Exclusive photographic reproduction of the beautiful pastoral, "Zooville at Midnight," the original of which was done in metal by Line O. Typer, member of L'Academie des Chambres de Composition. It will be noted that the lack of arms identifies the star as Venus, while the fact that the moon is upright shows that it is not full.

✧ ✧ ✧

NEW INVENTION

—Photo by Bunnell

Mrs. Mandy Lay, Sacred Cow of India, is here shown demonstrating her new invention, the pedestrian's tail light.

"Many of the roads through Balboa park have no sidewalks for pedestrians," Mrs. Lay explained, "and there is constant danger of them being hit by automobiles, which this invention will reduce. It has already been awarded the gold medal in the Safety First contest of the Cows' Anti Corned Beef association."

SAVANT

—Photo by Mehlin

Photographic study of Mr. Robert ("Bob") Katt, writer and bon vivant, author of "The Origin of The Bob," "What Made the Wildcat Wild," and other poems. Mr. Katt is here seen at work on his latest book, "Meat Eaters Have No Pimples."

✧ ✧ ✧

REVERSES THINGS

—Photo by Swope

"I always do get up at night, and dress by yellow candle light," says Teddibear, "and when it's day, I climb a tree and hit the hay. For day is made for sleepyheads to snooze serene in sunny beds; but when the night is black and dark—ah, then it's time to romp and lark!"

ZOO HISTORY*

ZOONOOZ and the Zoological Society of San Diego, here and now, extend a vote of thanks to W. B. France and the San Diego Sun for giving us the name of "ZOONOOZ." Mr. France coined this word while writing a zoo column for the above paper, and they have very generously granted us full title to it.

ZOONOOZ as it originally appeared in the San Diego Sun. Next page: ZOONOOZ, Volume 1, Number 1, 1926.

VOL. 1 JANUARY-FEBRUARY No. 1

SAN DIEGO
ZOONOOZ

PUBLISHED BY
THE ZOOLOGICAL SOCIETY OF SAN DIEGO
10 CENTS A COPY   FREE TO MEMBERS

Osa Johnson and Bong, a cheetah given by her to the San Diego Zoo.

side. Crews of volunteers worked like Trojans getting the necessary signatures on petitions to have the amendment put on the ballot. Two days before the deadline, the City Clerk advised us we were two thousand names under the required number. We garnered twenty earnest assistants and sent them out on the street with urgent pleas. By 11 o'clock of the day set for the deadline, we submitted our names to the City Clerk. He immediately called on the counters. All Saturday afternoon and Sunday they counted, but it was not until Monday morning when the Council ordered the amendment put on the ballot that we drew an easy breath.

All our troubles and worries were suitably crowned with a happy ending when the voters went to the polls on Election Day and voted us our 2-cent tax. And this time it stayed won.

Every once in a while, Balboa Park has an epidemic of some particular pest. First, it was Airedale dogs. Many San Diegans had adopted these as pets, and suddenly the whole tribe was smitten with a desire to hunt through the park. They invaded Pepper Grove and killed five of the deer that were kept there. Later, they chose the Zoo for their happy hunting ground. They would race outside the deer pens, barking so fiercely that several deer became panic-stricken and ran blindly into fences and trees and broke their necks. Then the Airedales took to climbing the seven-foot fence and attacking our kangaroos. At last, the Park authorities put an end to this destruction by the simple method of enforcing the law prohibiting dogs in the park unless leashed.

Cats were our second plague—one that has never subsided. Cats seem to enjoy a special immunity from our city pound, and innumerable stray cats have raised good-sized families in the park. Anybody who had an unwanted old mother cat about to present the world with kittens would put her in the car and dump her in Balboa Park. There the cat had to fend for its own food and so has preyed on the wild birds, as well as the food that we have provided for our Zoo animals. It seems strange that people who are so soft-hearted that they wouldn't send their cats to the Humane Society will abandon them to possible starvation.

In 1936, as a WPA project, we built a flying cage for birds of prey situated on the Monkey Mesa, on the opposite side from the cage for wading birds, and likewise settling in a canyon. In many cages, we have had instances of birds turning outlaw, leaving us no recourse but to kill them. In the bird-of-prey cage, one of them became so fierce that it attacked a keeper. In the wading cage, I have watched storks lie in wait for a small bird to happen along; and when it came, with a quick dart of its sharp bill, the stork would spear the innocent wayfarer and kill it.

In the fall of 1939, our educational work, which had been slowly recovering, made a noteworthy comeback. We regained possession of the Nevada Building and appointed a paid head to our Education Department. Also, our new, large capacious buses were made available to all city, county, and parochial schools. The bus called for the children at the school, took them around the Zoo with Mrs. Lena P. Crouse, head of our Education Department, telling them about the animals they passed and delivering them back to the school. In addition to this, during the summer Mrs. Crouse conducted classes in nature study for schoolchildren. So after twenty-three years of effort, our Education Department could boast all the equipment we had wanted for years—a building, a teacher, and transportation to and from schools.

(My secretary has been reading over the minutes of the Society's first meetings and remarks that they aren't very interesting, because all the discussions were about ways and

The birds of prey cage was billed as "the largest in the world" when it was completed in 1937. The small figure in front is Dr. Wegeforth.

means of raising money. Little she knows of the drama and comedy, the anxiety and rejoicing that lie behind those prosaic recordings! Personally, I think the struggle to finance the Zoo is one of the most exciting features of our growth; certainly, it is the keynote to the history of the Zoo's existence.)

Our normal procedure in financing was this: first, a project (such as the building of the monkey cages) was planned, down to the exact details of the construction. Next, the cost was carefully computed, and then we were smack up against the problem of financing the new undertaking. Our main reservoir, of course, was donations from well-to-do and public-spirited persons. I quickly learned that it was almost impossible to sell people on an exhibit still on paper; it took something concrete and tangible to exercise the necessary potent monetary appeal. We, therefore, frequently borrowed money from the bank for construction and then approached wealthy patrons for donations to pay off the loan, showing them the fine, new structure they would be giving to the children of San Diego.

We used similar tactics in buying animals, and our financial life was a two-noted existence of borrowing-the-money and paying-off-the-debt. Once we piled up a $31,000 debt by such loans. A wealthy and kindly friend paid off $15,000 and, in time, we liquidated the rest.

Only during the late thirties was the Zoo able to avoid large debts. This financial security was due largely to the increased attendance as the fame of the Zoo spread and to the special tax voted by the people of San Diego toward the support of the Zoo.

If in our early days we had had to budget our money as we were required to do later, undoubtedly we would still have been stumbling along, midget-size. The whole Zoo was a gamble from the start, but fortune usually favored us. Later, when we saw crowds coming in and exclaiming over our splendid collection, the fine, healthy condition of the animals, the beautiful grounds, we felt amply repaid for all the time and worry, the sacrifices and tribulations experienced all through the years.

PART THREE

THE ROAR GROWS LOUDER

by Neil Morgan

Dr. Wegeforth as a "San Diego Personality" in the San Diego Sun, *October 21, 1930.*

"Doctor Harry's" Ship Comes In

Just as the intensive plans of Harry Wegeforth have continued through the years since his death to facilitate the growth of the San Diego Zoo, his last animal-buying cruise brought tangible results to the Zoo two months after his death, in 1941. After a seventy-seven-day cruise across the Pacific, three elephants from India arrived at the Zoo in August 1941. They had been ordered by Wegeforth and Karl Koch on the 1940 trip to India, during which Wegeforth contracted pneumonia and malaria.

With the elephants were pygmy water buffalo, babirusa, civets, macaques, Hanuman monkeys, several hundred birds, and small animals ranging from cats to squirrels. One of the "prizes" of the shipment, a pair of snow leopards from the highest mountains of Tibet, had died in Calcutta before the ship sailed on its long voyage. War had begun to haunt the Pacific, and the voyage home, with Koch in charge of the shipment, was disturbed by uncertainty and secrecy.

With the elephants also came two Hindu youths to care for them. The boys became the absorbing new "exhibit" of the Zoo—on a thirty-day pass to this country—as charges of the Zoological Society. They were appalled at the prices of goods in this country and hoarded their earnings to buy gifts and goods when they would return to India. But their care for the three small elephants—Lucki, Little Maya, and Hari-Ki-Lash—was adequate, and then the Hindu lads were off for home again.

A month later, the Zoo took another strong step forward with the purchase of two female gorillas, through a $9,000 donation. They came from a group brought to New York by Henry Trefflich. For ten years, Wegeforth, Mrs. Benchley, and other Zoo officials had sought a permit to capture female mountain gorillas—the largest of the species—but Belgian authorities, jealous of their prize Belgian Congo species, were adamant. They were sought as mates for Mbongo and Ngagi. [In fact, Mbongo and Ngagi were later found to be eastern lowland gorillas.] Finally, Martin Johnson had written the Zoo that he had been promised a permit to collect two female gorillas for the San Diego Zoo, and that he would do so on his next trip. But Johnson was killed in a crash of a plane bringing him to Southern California.

The two females—named Kenya and Kivu—were released into their new homes at the San Diego Zoo, and several months after the death of Wegeforth began the great hope and experiment—that at last a gorilla might be born in captivity and live out a normal span of life.

Then, with the bombing of Pearl Harbor on December 7, 1941, the Zoo found itself on a precarious ledge incomparable to any that it had faced before. The Zoo was full of service personnel on that Sunday, and Zoo loud speakers blared forth an order to all servicemen to return to their ships and stations. Attendance dropped off abruptly because U.S. Army and Navy facilities surrounded the Zoo, blocked many roads, and tourist traffic fell to an absolute minimum. Defense building replaced Works Progress Administration construction at the Zoo. Yet because of increased income and attendance during the first 11 months of 1941, the grounds and buildings were in a condition never before equalled—and the collection of specimens in the Zoo was at an all-time peak.

In 1929, the "rolling stock" of the Zoo had consisted of a battered Model T Ford for hauling food through the grounds, a discarded, solid-tired, flat-rack truck used as a utility vehicle, and two Ford buses that heaved noticeably at the canyons and hills of the Zoo. By the start of World War II, the Zoo owned 14 automotive vehicles worth $20,000 and running some 4,000 miles a month in Zoo work. The three Zoo buses by this time carried about 46,000 passengers through the grounds each year.

After Pearl Harbor, Mrs. Benchley and her staff promptly prepared an emergency procedure to protect the 3,000 "citizens" of the Zoo and to guard against their outbreak. Shelters for most of the animals originally had been designed and built to be almost earthquake-proof, since that is what Wegeforth had presumed to be one of the gravest dangers in construction. The threat of air raid in the early months of World War II rapidly replaced earthquake, however, as the disaster most feared by the Zoo. The emergency procedure prescribed that each of the 35 men then on the Zoo staff would report immediately to the grounds in case of need, to supervise animals. Each man was equipped with a high-powered rifle and ordered to use it if necessary. Shutters were added to the large glass windows of the reptile house, and other buildings were strengthened where needed. Fortunately, the emergency procedure never was required.

That the Zoo survived the first, hysterical months after Pearl Harbor—economically and personnel-wise—was due to careful planning and organization and strong leadership. Zoos and parks throughout the West Coast were hard-hit by the war scare, and some others were closed.

Newspapermen who were on the staff of the *San Diego Union* in those months recall the telephone inquiry from a Santa Fe, New Mexico, telephone operator one night.

"This is the long-distance operator in Santa Fe," she said. "Is the San Diego Zoo open?"

The city editor said that it was.

"Thanks," the operator purred. "Friend of mine was just leaving for a vacation and thought she'd come out there if the Zoo were open!"

The Zoo Gears for War

The day of March 18, 1942, was sad at the Zoo.

Mbongo, then the largest gorilla in captivity, had been sick for three weeks. Mrs. Benchley had visited him several times each day, and he had responded affectionately

A familiar sight during the 1940s—lining up at the Zoo's entrance. While attendance dropped after the outbreak of World War II, it rose dramatically by the end of the decade.

most of that time. But finally his jet black coat began to lose its gloss and his eyes their luster. On March 18, at the age of 16, the great ape died that Martin and Osa Johnson had captured for the Zoo. He had been in his big cage at the Zoo for 10 years and 5 months. He had grown from 122 pounds to more than 600 pounds. Just the summer before, bronze busts of Mbongo and Ngagi had been completed and presented to the Zoological Society by Mrs. Harry M. Wegeforth. The busts are on display at this time near the ape cages. They are the work of Holger and Helen Jensen, who later did a bust of Harry Wegeforth, now in a niche at the Zoo's entrance.

But, as it is with any great Zoo, the shadow of death was pushed back by the brightness of birth. Days after the death of Mbongo came Raffy, the first giraffe to be born in the San Diego Zoo. Son of Patches, a giraffe from the highlands of Uganda, and Lofty, the

A Sunday afternoon scene, in the early 1950s, at the San Diego Zoo.

The bust of the great Ngagi (right) stands just inside the gates of the Zoo, along with that of Mbongo (below). Both bronzes were the work of Holger and Helen Jensen.

Photos courtesy of Holger Jensen.

new arrival was without human witnesses. Zoo officials had hoped to be present at the unusual event—but when the door of the enclosure was opened one morning, Raffy already was on hand and stood on unsteady legs for his first glance at human beings.

The career of Mbongo at the Zoo already had made scientific history. He and Ngagi did much to dispel the rumors of vicious ferocity that had up to that time surrounded the gorilla of fiction. As the ape thought closest in kin to the human, Mbongo himself showed timidity through his terror at a snake or camel when one appeared nearby.

An autopsy revealed that Mbongo was still young. He was still sexually immature, and his bones were not as hard as would have been expected in an adult gorilla. This led to the conclusion that the gorilla's span of life is comparable to that of man.

Many doctors and diagnosticians gave attention to the final illness that cost the life of Mbongo. It was a baffling disease. Neither his temperature nor respiration seemed seriously abnormal. Death was caused by a fungus, *Coccidioides immitis,* which had destroyed his lungs and spread to other organs. It is a fungus known to human beings and to cattle and frequently found at one time in the San Joaquin Valley of California. It was believed to have been contracted from soil or heavy dust.

Big news of the 1942 summer season at the Zoo was the development of an excellent elephant show by Jimmie O'Connor, a Consolidated Vultee Aircraft Corp. employee with valuable experience in animal training. Featuring the three, young Indian elephants ordered by Wegeforth and Koch, the show received its official "premiere" at the 26th annual meeting of the Zoological Society on August 3, 1942. The small elephants walked on a log, balanced and turned on it, and thoroughly amused the Society members and board with other stunts. The elephants then became an additional "act" in the daily sea lion and bear shows held in Wegeforth Bowl at the Zoo.

For the first time, the Zoo's own parking lot was established. New concrete and steel railings were added to the elephant pens. The bird yard was concreted and feed houses remodeled. As San Diego swelled to a booming wartime population, Zoo attendance began to increase again. New doors and paths were added to facilitate handling of the crowds. Almost 600,000 persons were admitted to the Zoo in the year ending June 30, 1942, a record attendance. The new load was made an acute problem by the quick turnover in experienced personnel caused by war and production demands. Public speaking demands on Mrs. Benchley, as executive secretary of the Zoo, increased; during that year she made 51 talks—including four to state and national conventions—and a series of 29 radio talks. Among the contributions of the Zoo to the war effort was a classic news photograph that was reprinted throughout the nation—showing Georgie the chimpanzee "weighing" his own toy, a rubber tire, as he was about to "turn it in" to the scrap-rubber drive.

Also bringing national and worldwide attention to the San Diego Zoo during this

Raffy, the first giraffe born at the San Diego Zoo, arrived in 1942. He was the son of Patches and Lofty.

Belle Benchley's books about her experiences at the Zoo would make it famous around the world.

Announcing...
MY LIFE in a Man-Made JUNGLE
by Belle J. Benchley

SAN DIEGO'S own Belle Benchley, the only woman zoo manager in the world, has just written one of the most original and entertaining books about animals ever published. Every reader of ZOONOOZ will find much of delight and interest in her experiences—ranging from "inside" stories of deadly rattlers-at-large, zoo courtships and zoo killers, to the problems of housekeeping and home-making for everything from a hippo to a humming bird. Such personalities as Bum, the condor, Marie, the smiling walrus, Sheik, the camel who went Hollywood, crowd the pages. There is fascinating information on the building of a zoo and the animal market. In themselves, the photographs are a rare treat.

MY LIFE IN A MAN-MADE JUNGLE
will be published on August 21 by Little, Brown & Co. ($3.00). We suggest that you will want to reserve your first edition (autographed if you wish) from us in advance.

STATIONERS CORPORATION
1040 SIXTH AVENUE   SAN DIEGO

Georgie the chimpanzee is shown here with his mother. He would later be seen in a classic newspaper photograph, "turning in" his toy tire to aid in the war's scrap-rubber drive.

period were the first two books to be written by the executive secretary and published by Little, Brown & Company—*My Life in a Man-Made Jungle* and *My Friends, the Apes*. Both books enjoyed critical acclaim and wide sales and did much to tell the world the story of the San Diego Zoo.

What apparently was the first condor to be hatched in captivity came to the Zoo on April 30, 1942. Its daddy was Bum, a fine bird measuring 10 feet from wing tip to wing tip. Bum had been brought to San Diego from the Hagenback Zoo in Hamburg, Germany, in 1928. The egg from which the chick hatched was incubated for 57 days, the male and female birds taking turns on the nest while the other stood guard.

Tragedy again struck the San Diego Zoo in February 1943, when Richard Havemann, noted Zoo animal trainer, died of wounds inflicted by a 3-year-old Himalayan bear that he had trained from a cub. For ten days, Havemann had fought to recover from deep claw wounds in his neck and back, which he received when he interceded to protect a carpenter from the attack of the frightened bear. Havemann's death was the first caused by an animal attack in the more than a quarter-century that the Zoo had been in operation.

Mickey the tapir with Mrs. Benchley and service personnel, c. 1940s.

By early 1943, the Zoo had adjusted itself handsomely to the exigencies of wartime operation. Answering the government's call to raise as much food as possible, several victory gardens were set up under the direction of Milton Leeper, superintendent of grounds. Swiss chard was grown for emus, alfalfa for birds, carrots and sweet corn for gorillas and other mammals—and peanuts, sweet potatoes, and other staple vegetables, which form a major part of the Zoo menu.

Gasoline and tire rationing threatened the Zoo's education program for children, placing Zoo buses in garages for some time. But Lena Crouse, chairman of the Zoo's Education Department, decided that if she couldn't bring schoolchildren to the Zoo, she would take the Zoo to the children—and did so, with a collection of hundreds of colored slides of Zoo animals and birds.

War brought its compensations. In World War I, the infant Zoo had been strengthened by contributions of bears and seals from U.S. Navy vessels—and by jungle animals brought up from Central America by U.S. Marines. Species began to drift in during World War II from all over the world, wherever the American G.I. found himself and remembered the Zoo of his hometown. From Asiatic and South Pacific jungles, and even from Africa, servicemen captured and shipped their contributions to the San Diego Zoo. Admiral W. F. Halsey informally expedited such shipments by Naval personnel on several occasions, mindful of the tremendous role of the San Diego Zoo in the amusement and instruction of the hundreds of thousands of military personnel training in, and in transit through, San Diego. On one occasion, a Consolidated Vultee pilot flew in a wallaby from Australia—a mere 36 flying hours away from his native haunts!

And another "compensation" of war was the invasion by the female of the last citadel of Men-Only at the Zoo—that of animal keeper. Georgia Dittoe, an attractive college graduate and veteran of animal show work, rolled up her sleeves one day at the Zoo when the man shortage was being worst felt, put on boots, and took over 20 cages of animals.

"I read Belle Benchley's book on the Zoo," she told inquiring reporters, "and heard that she needed some help. I was living in Los Angeles, so I packed up and came down and here I am!"

Georgia Dittoe, the Zoo's first woman keeper, with a lesser panda. She had been inspired by Mrs. Belle Benchley's books about the San Diego Zoo.

150   THE NEW "FIRST TEAM"

Puddles the hippo, 1945, with Keeper Ken Howard and servicemen. Former Keeper "Tex" McRorey is seen in uniform, to the right of Ken Howard

The New "First Team"

The "old-timers"—who conceived the idea of the San Diego Zoo—were all gone by 1943. The last of the original group of five founders was Dr. J. C. Thompson, who in 1916 was stationed with the Navy in San Diego and was one of the group who answered Dr. Harry Wegeforth's call for help. Dr. Thompson died on March 7, 1943, in San Francisco. He had done much in planning the education program of the Zoo and had directed nature walks through the Zoo. On his last visit to San Francisco, Wegeforth had visited with Dr. Thompson—and reviewed the years of the conception of the San Diego Zoo.

But the new "first team" was performing capably.

At this time, Lester T. Olmstead was president. Mrs. Benchley was continuing the service she began in 1926 as executive secretary. Other officers and members of the board in

THE NEW "FIRST TEAM"   151

1942-43 were F. L. Annable, Gordon Gray, Fred Kunzel, T. M. Russell, Mrs. Robert P. Scripps, C. L. Cotant, J. Waldo Malmberg, W. C. Crandall, Robert Sullivan, Milton Wegeforth (son of the founder), and Dr. T. O. Burger.

Annual attendance wavered between 500,000 and 600,000 through most of the war, hampered always by tire and gas rationing—and increased by the hundreds of military personnel brought in groups to visit the Zoo by their officers-in-charge. Though the war crippled the market for surplus Zoo specimens, thus decreasing one type of income, the increasing paid attendance made the Zoo budget equal to rising food costs and expenses.

There was a shift in emphasis that typified the war problems: two horses that had been marked for slaughter and feed were reprieved, to pull a plow in the victory garden.

The necessity for economy in food and manpower during war operations led to a gradual decrease in the number of specimens on exhibit at the Zoo. By June 1943, there were 653 animals, 1,407 birds, and 556 reptiles—2,616 specimens, intentionally the smallest inventory in several years.

A rare service of nursing to a rare animal—Ngagi, the giant eastern lowland gorilla whose companion Mbongo had lost his life through a fungus infection—was performed by Byron Moore at this time. Ngagi became ill just as Mbongo had—and with no known medical treatment, Moore spent each night for four weeks returning to the Zoo at 10 p.m. to give Ngagi a pan of warm milk and some comforting attention to assure him he was not neglected. With such persistent nursing, Ngagi survived this illness.

The vital statistics of Zoo operation continued unabated—a baby hippopotamus born in October 1943, named Little Lotus, the first in the Zoo; a world record set by a black cobra for longevity of cobras in captivity, this one living at the Zoo from 1928; and the hatching and raising of a goura, the rare Victoria crowned pigeon.

Not covered by such vital statistics, however, are the love and understanding that Zoo people—and often the public—lavish on the animals within their care. As Mrs. Benchley wrote in ZOONOOZ, after observing the infant habits of Little Lotus, the Zoo's first baby hippopotamus:

> Mother affection is always a touching thing, and the ways that animal mothers have of showing their tender feelings has been a never failing source of delight to me. This mother (Ruby) turns and puts her great lips, which could easily cover more than half her baby, against the little head. Often when eating she leaves its face comically covered with green alfalfa. I have never heard either of them make a sound to each other, but they have a clever way of pushing on the proper foot with the heavy mouth and indicating that a step in the right direction is needed . . . .

Just in time for Christmas, 1943, came another delicate "first"—the first baby zebra born at the San Diego Zoo, named Thunder because he was born at the height of a thunderstorm, rare in San Diego.

Not even intent nursing could prolong much longer the life of the great gorilla Ngagi, who had exceeded the normal life span of a captured gorilla by many times. In January 1944, Ngagi became critically ill and, after two weeks, died. Coronary thrombosis caused death. Ngagi died at a weight of 639 pounds, probably in excess of the final weight of Mbongo. Now the Zoo was left with Kenya, the female lowland gorilla. Kivu, who had come to the Zoo with Kenya, already had passed away. At that, Kenya was the only gorilla on display in any western American zoo.

In midsummer of 1944, a rare inhabitant reached the Zoo, and behind its arrival was one of the more intricate stories of World War II liaison. It was a kagu bird, one of the rarest of all species, which had been presented by the people of New Caledonia to Admiral William F. Halsey, in appreciation of his fleet's defense of that area in the opening months of World War II. With the kagu, Halsey received an export permit, which made the bird the first to be brought to the United States in many years. One of the few already in the country was on display at the San Diego Zoo and awaited its new friend. Not much larger than a seagull, the kagu was mauve in color and resembled a small heron. But the Navy and Admiral Halsey had no use for the kagu. That's how a committee of three—two Waves and a Navy chief—were sent by Admiral Halsey to escort the kagu to the San Diego Zoo, where it was checked in as a regular guest.

Zoo, I Love You!

The San Diego Zoo, always a dependable source of "color" for Hollywood film producers, appeared again on the cinema screens of the world in the fall and winter of 1944. From the scraggly, unhappy hyena that Harry Wegeforth had sold to a filmmaker just after World War I—for a sum that helped feed the Zoo at a crucial time—the contribution of the Zoo to Hollywood had grown substantially.

This time, the Zoo appeared in a Universal Pictures feature called, "San Diego, I Love You." *Time* gave a major bow to the Zoo when it reviewed the picture:

> [This is] a cheerfully goofy little picture about a bad inventor who made good, and is almost as funny as it is foolish.... Louise Allbritton takes Jon Hall to San Diego's Zoo where, with very sensible leisure, the camera forgets all about the plot to watch a couple of engaging bears, hindfeet clasped in paws, rock back and forth on their bottoms. The bears are probably the best thing in the show ....

Of more significance to the Zoo staff, and at the same time, was the tour of the San Diego Zoo by officials of the New York Zoological Society. Fairfield Osborn, president of the Society, made his first visit to the San Diego Zoo, and his praise was effervescent:

> The San Diego Zoo has won an international reputation for its outstanding exhibit of birds and animals, and its influence is felt wherever zoos are maintained. Your zoo has gained fame throughout the land for taking the lead in establishment of a research unit in connection with its exhibits, and I believe much has been added to the sum of human medical knowledge as a result of this scientific work. I know that other zoos, including our own, are very impressed with this program, and are now following your lead.

The Zoo continued, even during the height of the war, to put into effect new developments and projects that long had been in the minds of Harry Wegeforth and of Mrs. Benchley. In 1944, a cherished dream of Wegeforth's was fulfilled when a second gate was opened at the main entrance to the Zoo—a move made necessary by the tremendous Sunday crowds coming to that gate by the trolleys, which soon were to be erased from the San Diego scene. Daily crowds began to set new records—such as the 7,755 visitors on February 14, 1944. At this time the first official Zoo guidebook was published. It had been in preparation for several years—much of it having been read and approved by Harry Wegeforth before his death.

Through the efforts of Lt. John Burke of the Navy, an unusual shipment of birds reached the Zoo in 1944 from the Solomon Islands. None of the species previously had been represented in the San Diego Zoo, and few of them were known in American markets and zoos. They included eclectus parrots, cockatoos, lories, hornbills, and Nicobar pigeons.

Bus tours came back to the Zoo in 1945, following a period of gas rationing.

The year of 1944 also brought the birthday of a famed giraffe—D-Day, born June 6 while the Allied armed forces were launching the historic invasion of the European continent. D-Day was a brother to Raffy, born in the Zoo two years before. Like Raffy, he was a frisky youngster from birth. D-Day brought national publicity once again to the Zoo. Other notable births during 1944 included a Grevy's zebra, a Chinese muntjac, an Anubis baboon, and a Hanuman langur.

Because of wartime suspensions on building for such projects as zoos, building plans were put aside—including construction of the Wegeforth Memorial Educational Building, which was being planned at the time of Wegeforth's death.

But one vital bit of building was done. The iron pillars and wires of Trudy's cage were strengthened and extended. For Trudy, the Zoo's elusive tapir, had outsmarted her keepers three times. Brought to the Zoo in 1940 from Malaya, Trudy made headlines frequently. Certainly not a beautiful or graceful animal, Trudy didn't seem belligerent either; but she was restless. Her most publicized escape set off a week-long search of the Park and city—with Zoo officials convinced that an animal of her size couldn't simply drop out of sight within the city. But that is actually what Trudy had done. A city worker had stepped down into a flood sewer to check it—and, in the light of his flashlight, had been confronted suddenly with what he was convinced was a rhinoceros. It was obviously impossible to remove Trudy through any nearby opening, and so Zoo keepers studied city maps to find an opening in the underground channel through which she could be brought out. This led to the astonishing discovery that Trudy had entered the sewer in the Park and walked about a mile in the general direction of the bay. She was forced around and finally brought out into the light of Balboa Park, never to roam the city again.

With 1945 came a new annual attendance record at the Zoo—a total recorded attendance of 652,468 for the year ending with June 1945. Yet the big goals were being set for postwar years. San Diego Brownie girls made their annual visit to the Zoo and for the second year added money to a Gorilla Fund started by children from the Convalescent Home, who hoped to see another gorilla added to the Zoo at the close of war. The third successful volume written by the executive secretary was published, *My Animal Babies,* and won praise from critics. "Duck Island" was built amid the Zoo pond, and a new group of small mammal cages was added. Postwar construction plans were laid for a new combined administration and cafe building, elephant compound, and small mammal house. But funds for construction were to remain a bugaboo in the path of vital development.

Gas rationing was relaxed enough by the fall of 1945 to allow the Zoo to put back into service its familiar buses, touring the Zoo. The tour, as reinstated, consumed an hour and was accompanied by a running lecture by Ken Howard—concerning many of the more than 2,500 birds and animals of the Zoo.

Herpetology and research had a unique blending one winter day in 1945 at the Zoo, when new, portable X-ray equipment added to the Research Hospital was used to take the first X-ray pictures of a python in captivity. The occasion was that C. B. Perkins, Zoo herpetologist, noted the serpent coiled in an unnatural position and found his rear section partially paralyzed. Perkins found a python more difficult to X-ray than a human being, because his skin is—photographically—three times as difficult to penetrate as human skin. Thus, a triple-length time exposure was required.

Not in the nature of "big events," but human and typical of the day-to-day life of zoo people, are these excerpts from a "diary" kept by Mrs. Belle Benchley during 1945. They are significant neither as headlines nor history, but as a reflection of the deep love of animals so inherent in a fine zoo staff:

Jan. 2: Our first baby of the year, a cunning little brown bundle born to good old Susie, the European brown bear.

Jan. 18: Stark tragedy struck the cat canyon today. The male of our old pair of leopards, which had raised many young and lived harmoniously for years, suddenly attacked and killed his mate.

Feb. 2: This was a busy day for the stork. First, a baby black lutong was born; then Dottie, our white female llama, gave birth to her first baby. The father was John, our famous "spitting llama." The baby monkey lived only by the special care of Moore and Arnold.

April 14: A few animals are coming through from Africa and South America. We had ordered a few monkeys to fill out some of our groups. Today we received two Sykes' monkeys.

May 12: This is the annual festival of the "Bluebirds" (children's organization). 348 took part in lovely ceremonies at the Wegeforth Bowl.

May 26: 1,054 Brownie Scouts came in today. They have been coming now for at least ten years.

July 24: Broke one of our fast rules against taking care of any animal that belongs to anyone else when we let some "returnee" marines bring 28 tiny Philippine macaques to the Zoo Hospital, where we will care for them until the boys are discharged and can take them home.

October 16: I left for San Antonio to attend conference of zoo directors regarding an Australian exchange. Baby hippo (male) born at 1:30 p.m.

December 21: Admiral Ingram sent us two beautiful macaws to take care of for him until he is ashore again. They are his pets.

December 31: Total attendance for year, 702,746!

Mrs. Benchley enters the Zoo cafe, 1936, which was also the Zoo entrance.

Part of Coming Out of the War

By the spring of 1946, the postwar era seemed to have begun for zoos, particularly for the San Diego Zoo. For the first time, along the San Diego Embarcadero, after five years, the coughing bark of sea lions was heard—when the fishing craft *Two Sisters* arrived with a cargo of 38 of the animals, captured offshore at the Coronado Islands for the Zoo.

The Zoo in prewar years had imported thousands of the "seals" for exchange with zoos throughout the world and had supplied virtually all the "seals" seen in American circuses. The sea lion found in waters south of Santa Barbara is believed to be the only sea lion that can be trained.

The increasing exchange of animals had an interesting highlight in the shipment of the San Diego Zoo's giraffe, Raffy, to the San Francisco Zoo. The San Diego giraffe family had been growing so speedily that somebody had to go—and San Francisco wanted Raffy. He was trucked northward along the California coast—standing backwards in his trailer—to solace the grief of a lady giraffe whose mate had died recently. Carey Baldwin, director of the San Francisco Zoo, had quite a problem in shipping Raffy. He paid $4,000 for the animal, then fought its recalcitrant nature for three days, striving to get Raffy into a low-built truck that stood by at $5 per hour.

Barely had Raffy reached San Francisco when he had a new brother, born in the San Diego Zoo. Schoolchildren voted on the name for "Master X"—and the newborn giraffe promptly was dubbed "Rusty."

Postwar days brought calls from European zoos for help in reestablishing their collections. The San Diego Zoo was able to answer an S.O.S. from the London Zoo for reptiles to refill their war-emptied snake pits. San Diego youths helped answer the call by bringing in native snakes, which were shipped to London along with Zoo specimens.

Another postwar innovation within Zoo grounds was the first summer season of the San Diego Civic Light Opera Association, which opened its historic career with a production of "The Mikado" in the Wegeforth Bowl. Robert J. Sullivan, president of the Association, later was to become president of the Zoological Society, continuing his strong interest in Zoo and civic affairs that stemmed from his early association with Dr. Harry Wegeforth.

Sadness came to the annual meeting of the Zoological Society on August 5, 1946, when Albert J. Jones, a charter member of the Society, collapsed and died while attending the meeting. All reports and speeches were cancelled. All officers were reelected: Charles L. Cotant, president; L. M. Klauber, vice president; John P. Scripps, second vice president; Fred Kunzel, secretary; Robert J. Sullivan, treasurer; and W. C. Crandall, Milton Wegeforth, Klauber, and Sullivan as directors.

Back from the war came some of the familiar animal keepers and aides to the Zoo, prominent among the aides being Ken Stott, Jr., who had represented the Zoo even as a Navy man in the Pacific—writing regular features for ZOONOOZ, on his animal and bird observations in the tropics, and facilitating occasional shipments of specimens to the Zoo. Stott had begun his Zoo career as a writer in his early high school days. Also back to the Zoo staff came Charles Shaw, herpetologist, who promptly departed for Arizona and northwest Sonora and brought more than 60 reptile specimens back to the Zoo. K. C. Lint returned from the Philippines to his post as aide in the bird department.

Of vital importance to postwar development was announcement of a grant by the Ellen Browning Scripps Foundation to the Zoological Society's Biological Research Institute and Zoological Hospital. The funds were for research in fields of bacteriology, parasitology, pathology, and related aspects of vital interest to the Zoo. The grant perpetuated, after her death, the tremendous interest and aid for the Zoo that had characterized Miss Scripps.

A fine camel pen was added in these postwar months, and fences that had been wearing for 20 years gradually were replaced.

Ken Stott, Jr., later to become the Zoo's general curator, served in the U.S. Navy during the Second World War. While stationed in the Pacific he wrote articles for ZOONOOZ on his bird and animal observations.

In 1946, indicating the vast physical growth of the Zoo, Ralph Virden, maintenance superintendent, summarized these changes: in 1930, there had not been a single electric motor in use on Zoo grounds; sixteen years later, there were 60 such motors in operation each day. In 1930, there had been one telephone; in 1946, 15 phones. Automotive equipment, plumbing facilities, and shop equipment showed similar startling growth.

In feeding, the complex problems of Zoo menus became more and more intricate as the Zoo grew. There was Mike the orangutan who had an ulcer in his throat and ate avocados because they were soft. There were the Mexican rattlers, who needed a dead rat or two every once in a while. And Gertie, the 150-odd-year-old tortoise, was partial to cactus. Giraffes like dried onions and acacia limbs, with some tea leaves occasionally tossed in for spice. Horsemeat is the staple—three horses a week consumed on the average during the postwar years, and hundreds of pounds of fresh vegetables and fruits, and fish. But the San Diego Zoo—with its 25-man kitchen staff—has all along had many benefits that other zoos seldom can acquire. Many native shrubs and trees—and thus native habitat diets—can be grown in the temperate San Diego climate. Much of the

K. C. Lint, the Zoo's popular curator of birds, first started his work as an aide in the bird department.

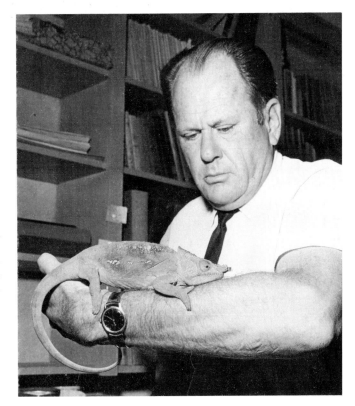

Charles Shaw, herpetologist, returned to the Zoo after the war and promptly departed on a trip that resulted in more than 60 reptile specimens brought back for exhibit.

menu of the San Diego Zoo has been possible—naturally—because of the planning over many decades in bringing botanical specimens from all over the world.

The Zoo is Famed

The year 1947 brought new records to the San Diego Zoo.

Gate admissions soared to 734,975. New purchases of animals swelled the population of the Zoo. More than ever before, national publicity brought attention to the San Diego Zoo. Discussion of the Zoo came in such magazines as *The Saturday Evening Post, Time, Look,* and *Science News Letter.* In a notable *Time* layout of American zoos, 7 of the 21 color photographs were made at the San Diego Zoo. Distinguished visitors from zoos and natural history museums throughout the world visited the San Diego Zoo, as travel restrictions from wartime were lifted completely. Paramount Pictures came to the Zoo to film animals for a movie "short." And "Lena II," a striped hyena from Arabia, made headlines halfway around the world as she arrived in New York by ship and came to the San Diego Zoo by chartered plane.

There were setbacks, too. "Captain" Wesley C. Crandall, who joined the Zoological Society in 1917, even before its incorporation was complete, passed away. He had been a close friend of the Zoo throughout his years as a member of the City Council, Park Commission, a president and member of the Society's board of directors, a close friend of Harry Wegeforth, and then as executive secretary and director of the Ellen Browning Scripps Foundation. He had been a major personal factor in establishing the Zoo research fellowships through that Foundation.

Dr. Arthur L. Kelly, a graduate of the School of Veterinary Medicine at the University of Kansas, arrived at the Zoo in February 1947, to assume the position of Zoo Veterinarian and that of Director of Research at the Biological Institute. He was the first full-time veterinarian since the resignation of Dr. Frank McKinney from the Zoo staff in 1943. During the interim, the burden had been carried by Mrs. Emily Burlingame, an Estonian native with a brilliant medical background in Mexico City and subsequently in San Diego. With the arrival of Dr. Kelly, the Scripps Fellowships were placed in motion and medical men began to give especial attention to research matters in the Zoo facilities.

One interesting outgrowth of Zoo research work in animal medicine was the accumulation of autopsy reports. Generalized over the years, these show causes of death that follow fixed patterns. Small birds, for example, were found to have died most frequently from mechanical injuries—fear-crazed flights into wall or wire. Free-flying birds or ground birds like peacocks, pigeons, and jungle fowl met death more often by unwise venturing within reach of a monkey cage, or from flying into a lion grotto. Pneumonia and digestive disorders became major death factors with the larger birds. Gout and

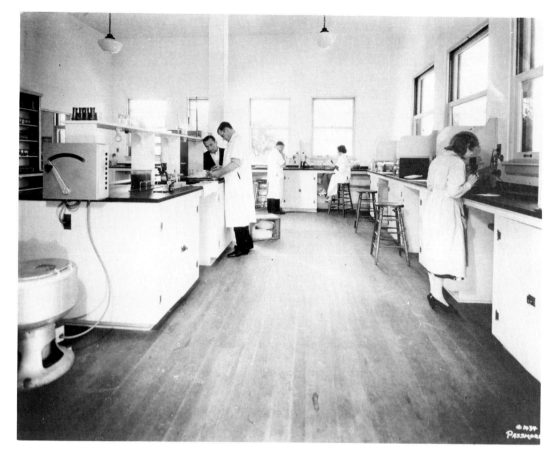

The interior of the Zoo's hospital. Work and records completed here over the years were beginning to pay off by the late 1940s, with a better understanding of the needs and care of captive animals.

tuberculosis figure in these deaths also.

With reptiles, strangely, until construction of the glass-fronted cages, one major cause of death was man: poking sticks, tapping fingers, or faces thrust so close to a screen as to make the highly nervous serpent injure himself. An equally significant cause of reptile death was found to be digestive disorder, often caused by injured mouths. But there always are the freak cases: a boa constrictor with enteritis, or inflammation of the intestine, a water moccasin with ulcers, and three turtles with tumors.

Fatalities among the mammals were found to be from varied causes. The nervous antelope is more likely to die from fear-crazed mechanical injury. Digestive troubles predominate in deaths of seals, sea lions, and walrus. Among primates, monkeys and apes are found to have the widest variety of causes of death—including appendicitis, gallstones, heat stroke, rupture, and coronary thrombosis, many of them as parallel to human disease as the theory of evolution would lead the scientist to suspect.

A new chapter in Zoo development opened in August 1947, with the addition to the Zoo collection of the only four northern fur seals in captivity. The Zoo previously had established longevity records for this species, following the donation in 1935 of five specimens by the Bureau of Fisheries. The longest survivor endured nine years of captivity—in comparison with a previous record of mere months. The four northern fur seals added to the Zoo collection in 1947 had been captured shortly before at the Northwest Point rookery on St. Paul Island and were brought from the Pribilofs through the efforts of U. S. Fisheries officials. The arrival was hailed by Zoo officials, because since its earliest days, the San Diego Zoo had featured marine mammals, especially the sea lions taken in Baja California and Southern California waters. Karl W. Kenyon, a native San Diegan then in the employ of the Fur Seal Commission in a research capacity, aided in the capture and shipment of the four mammals.

A particularly timely news development of the summer of 1947 was the screaming headline: "HITLER SHOT AND KILLED." It was, however, an unfortunate headline because the Hitler referred to was a beloved, 800-pound Russian brown bear who in 12 years had become one of the Zoo's best-liked animals. He escaped from Bear Grotto through a prankster's stunt—and when hunted down became excited and bolted. It finally became necessary to shoot and kill the bear.

More than 30 zoo directors from the nation's major cities toured the San Diego Zoo in the fall of 1947 as a side trip from the San Francisco convention of the American Association of Zoological Parks and Aquariums. Here are some of the comments they made to newspaper reporters:

> Freeman Shelley, Philadelphia Zoo: "This Zoo in San Diego is doing things that are possible only in San Diego! Animals in the open all year around—and look at those flowers!"
> George P. Vierheller, director, St. Louis Zoo: "I never tire of coming here to gain new ideas."
> Lee Crandall, general curator, New York Zoological Park: "I've seen things I don't believe; animals almost running loose—specimens of nature I never have seen outside of a museum."
> Fletcher Reynolds, Cleveland Zoo: "San Diego has the world's ideal zoo, and the finest group of rare animals, displayed in an incomparable, natural setting."

In May 1948, Ken Stott, Jr., as general curator of the Zoological Society, left San Diego on a four-month tour of Africa to make contacts for the San Diego Zoo with zoo, museum, and conservation officials of Africa. A side purpose of his trip was to study African animals and birds in their natural habitats, attempting to learn better how to keep and exhibit animals at the San Diego Zoo.

By June 30 of that year, with Zoo attendance having topped the 800,000 mark for the previous fiscal year, the executive secretary concluded in her annual report that the San Diego Zoo had reached a delicate point of maturity:

> The looked-for drop following the heavy war period attendance, both civilian and military, has not materialized.... We have not yet reached that saturation point of some of the older zoos

nor the place where any of our installations are so obsolete that they must be completely discarded. We do not have to refuse to exhibit some of the most attractive exhibits because they are common or cheap. But we do have to choose carefully so as not to overstock and to keep the Zoo within a scope that can be fairly well seen in a one day's visit....

Big News and Gorillas

There is a tremendous difference between "big news" to zoo people and "big news" to the zoo-going public. The forced feeding of a python drew thousands to the Zoo during the twenties, but it was routine procedure to Zoo helpers. In the same way, matters that approach crowning achievements for Zoo initiates may hold little or no interest for the public.

It was virtually that way with two historic births that occurred at the San Diego Zoo during 1948: the first Alaskan fur seal to be born in any American zoo, and the first blesbok antelope born in captivity in western America.

Like buffalo, the blesboks, medium-sized antelopes, once were common in middle and southern Africa, roaming in huge herds. Gradually, they were almost exterminated by hunters. They are found today only in game preserves and zoos.

The fur seal pup was a carbon copy of its parents, which had come the year before from the Pribilof Islands seal herd in the Bering Sea. It heightened interest in the Zoo collection as it was the only Alaskan fur seal group on display anywhere in the world at that time.

Steadily, the Zoo was building up its collection of the rare and macabre. A pair of Egyptian shoebills [storks], native to an isolated section of the Nile River, reached the Zoo in March 1948. Days later, climaxing Zoo efforts of more than 20 years, a wicked-looking trio of kea birds arrived from New Zealand. These are the "varmints" so hated by the sheepherders of New Zealand, because of their deadly attacks on sheep. The herders wiped out almost all of the kea birds in a concentrated drive, and the few remaining—as long as the herders have anything to do with it—are destined to be zoo specimens.

One of the happier additions of this time was a five-year-old female orangutan, Doris—who was an immediate favorite with Zoo staffers and visitors and the culmination of a long search for a mate for Kokok, the Zoo's male orang.

K. C. Lint, curator of birds at the San Diego Zoo, undertook during the summer of 1948 to "hand raise" the first female Andean condor hatched at the San Diego Zoo. Behind the birth lay a strange story. The first condor hatched in captivity in America, from an artificially incubated egg, had been a male at the San Diego Zoo, in 1942. This specimen of the giant bird was sent to the National Zoological Park in Washington.

Scientists then believed that condors laid only one egg every two years. The second chick was hatched almost exactly two years later at the Zoo. It went to Salt Lake City. In 1947, still on schedule, another male condor arrived. But then early in 1948, the parent condors began their colorful courting dance—during which they will not tolerate the presence of their young. At this time the third offspring was sent to the San Antonio Zoo. Zoo officials in San Diego settled back to study the strange speedup in the birth of their condors.

The nesting progressed normally, and the condor arrived—theoretically a year ahead of schedule—and the existing scientific pattern was broken. Strange, too, was to see the baby without the comb or wattle. Promptly, Zoo officials realized they had another stroke of history—the first female condor hatched in captivity in San Diego. That is when Lint braved the fury of the parent birds to take the chick away from them and begin to raise it without their help, thinking that perhaps this would reveal further evidence of the nesting and birth cycle.

The San Diego Zoo made new friends on New Year's Day of 1949 when the city of San Diego entered a floral portrayal of the Zoo in the Tournament of Roses parade at Pasadena. The float won a second prize in the Class A Division for municipalities. Four wide-eyed and entranced children were depicted observing polar bears, zebras, lions, tigers, Rocky Mountain bighorn sheep, and monkeys.

Two days later, like a small Noah's ark, a truckload of animals left the San Diego Zoo with its ultimate destination the zoo in Auckland, New Zealand. It was the largest shipment made by the San Diego Zoo since before World War II. Notable was the fact that all of the animals except the sea lions and one puma had been born at the San Diego Zoo. The shipment was in return for keas, paradise ducks, and pukekos—a rare New Zealand swamp fowl. The Zoo was pushing plans for construction of a new administration building, a dream delayed by war and postwar adjustments, and for an elephant building and a small mammal building. Plans had been drawn for the three structures. In the spring of 1949, an estimated cost of $627,871 was placed on the three buildings. The matter was being handled through city council channels and with hope that the State of California would provide "matching funds" to make possible the construction. Cost studies continued throughout 1949.

Now without any gorilla, the San Diego Zoo and its secretary, Mrs. Benchley, had become extremely gorilla-conscious. More than $5,000 had been builtup in a public fund launched by children, toward the purchase of gorillas. In the summer of 1949, bitter disappointment came to Mrs. Benchley. Six gorillas were being brought by plane from French West Africa to New York and, through French zoo friends, she had been able to secure an option to buy a pair for San Diego. It was Mrs. Benchley's hope that if two

The Zoo's big news for 1949 was the arrival of a male and two female gorillas named Albert, Bouba, and Bata.

baby gorillas could be started in captive life together, for the first time a gorilla "family" could be developed within captivity. But like so many reports in animal dealing, the report of these arriving gorillas was exaggerated. The new arrivals were all tiny babies, weighing under eight pounds each, and each less than six months old. It seemed obvious to Mrs. Benchley and others at the Zoo that these were too young either for display or for any good chance that they could be successfully reared at the Zoo. So the hopes for gorilla rearing seemed destined for another delay. But Mrs. Benchley began to brood over the possibility of missing a rare chance—and when Dr. Arthur Kelley, Zoo veterinarian, passed through New York several weeks later on his way to a London convention, she suggested that he stop by and look at the gorillas. He found them in remarkably good health.

Then, remembering Ngagi and Mbongo—and that the Zoo had been without a gorilla since the death of Kenya, in 1947—Mrs. Benchley decided to make another effort at recapturing the Zoo's old title of "Gorilla Capital." She bought a male and two females. Out they came with Miss Sadie Taylor, longtime animal "mother" for Animal Dealer

Henry Trefflich, in "attendance" with the three babies. The three babies drew a Zoo crowd of 10,000 persons on the first day they went on public display, a new record for attendance. Though they arrived at the Zoo with colds, they made quick recoveries under the careful nursing of Miss Taylor and San Diego Zoo keepers. Congo, later renamed Albert, turned out to be seven months old; Oka and Lady Congo were eight and nine months old, respectively. They were later renamed Bata and Bouba.

In the years since, the San Diego Zoo has become famed again for its gorillas. One of the most interesting developments of the successful acclimation of Albert, Bata, and Bouba was the visit to the Zoo of Dr. Robert M. Yerkes, Yale University psychobiology professor emeritus, who undertook a long sequence of study to determine, in part, whether the apes could be taught to "talk." Through close study of the gorillas, he believed he could devise improved methods even of educating human beings. His experiments at the San Diego Zoo involved efforts to give the gorillas, if not actual words, at least symbolic sounds as a basis for further training and "talk."

One of the most humorous columns written by Hal Boyle, Associated Press staffer, concerned the three gorillas and Professor Yerkes' experiments. He wrote, "Suppose all three gorillas turn out to be mental wizards. I still can see nothing but trouble ahead for them. If Albert learns to spell "Africa" at the age of 3, won't he at 12 be asking why he can't go to Yale and become the first gorilla to win a college degree? Boy, what a halfback he'd be—he'd make Frank Merriwell look like a monkey!"

During his two-month stay with the gorillas, Dr. Yerkes reported some progress, with the aid of Edalee Orcutt Harwell, who spoon-fed the baby gorillas and taught them to obey simple commands such as "No," 'Sit down," and "Lie down."

The love and excitement that gorillas brought back to the San Diego Zoo was typified, however, in the smiling remarks that Belle Benchley made so spontaneously as she watched the babies in their indoor playpen: "Why, Ngagi used to do that!" Or, "I've seen Mbongo in just that pose!"

The Animals are the Show

With Albert, Bata, and Bouba thriving and happy, Belle Benchley—now world-famed after 24 years with the San Diego Zoo—headed for Europe in 1950 to join zoo directors from all over the world at a London conference. As Harry Wegeforth had done decades before, she practiced some shrewd "horse" trading, too—using sea lions for "bait." She had been honored during the forties with many titles and awards—and immediately upon her return to San Diego she was given the Woman of the Year award by the San Diego Soroptimist Club. This was civic acclaim; long before, she had been acclaimed within the zoo fraternity as the first zoo official west of the Mississippi to be elected president of the American Association of Zoological Parks and Aquariums.

Young Albert and Edalee Orcutt Harwell with statue of Ngagi, 1951.

The "Botany Bay" koalas, 1952, with Zoo Director Mrs. Benchley, Veterinarian Glen Crosbie, and General Curator Ken Stott, Jr.

During her European tour she still sought gorillas, and she conferred with Belgium officials about the possibility of trapping a pair of mountain gorillas for the San Diego Zoo.

The annual meeting of the Zoological Society on August 8, 1950, was the occasion for a look backwards at the progress of the Zoo. One result was the announcement that a free-admission "Wegeforth Day" was to be set up at the Zoo each October 2—then 34 years from the day the first Zoo organization meeting was held at the instigation of Harry Wegeforth.

All attendance records were revealed once more to have been broken during the 1949-1950 year, with 915,288 attending the Zoo. As Mrs. Benchley pointed out:

> Our triumphs as the Zoo grows older seem much more modest. They come with security, success and an established income. Highlights of later years have been our first baby hippo and giraffes, three young gorillas, the breeding of condors and ocellated turkeys, the attendance mark, and finally the constant reminder that the Zoo is one of the great institutions, not only of this continent but of the world; and that it is no longer a follower but a leader and a power in the fields of science and education. It grew from a small seed, only because of herculean efforts of a few people, begun when our city was a town and our park largely a pasture.

The first Dr. Harry Wegeforth Free Day, in October 1950, was a unique tribute to the founder of the Zoo. The number of visitors was not unusually large, but it was a surprising group of visitors. Some had traveled far. Some had not been to the Zoo for years. Many of them had been close friends of Harry Wegeforth, people close to him in building the Zoo—some who had given money, some who had given massive effort, all at the Zoo to pay him tribute and to exchange stories of the "old days"—and the new.

By the next summer of 1951, Zoological Society directors were able to hear a report that proved again the Zoo was fulfilling its function: for the first time, annual attendance exceeded the million mark. Over 1,125,000 persons went through Zoo gates during the 1950-51 fiscal year. In his retiring report as Society president, Laurence Klauber stated that the Zoo "plant" had been appraised at $1,484,000 in value, and the animals conservatively valued at $330,000. Klauber was succeeded as president at this meeting by one of the youngest heads of the Zoological Society in history—38-year-old Robert J. Sullivan, another longtime protégé of Harry Wegeforth.

But the story of the Zoo is its animals. It was proven vividly to the Zoo staff again when even Albert, Bata, and Bouba were shoved out of the national limelight with the arrival of four, fetching Australian koalas.

Aside from being termed one of the greatest single coups in zoo-keeping history, the procuring of the koalas was vivid evidence of the persuasive powers of Belle Benchley who, like Harry Wegeforth, wouldn't be stopped. For 25 years she had been beseeching

Dr. Wegeforth's grandson, Harry G. Wegeforth, poses with one of the Zoo's new koalas, in 1952.

Australian authorities to allow koalas out of their country for the San Diego Zoo. When finally the little charmers arrived, it was through a special act of the Australian Parliament, allowing exportation of the koalas solely to the San Diego Zoo.

And the story of the koalas also brought to a symbolic climax the shrewd, patient planning of the leaders in building the Zoo and the strong bond of continuous effort represented first by Harry Wegeforth and, later, by Mrs. Belle Benchley.

The Australian embargo on exportation of the koala was in deference to the animal's finicky eating habits. Certain types of eucalyptus trees provide its only diet. Twenty-five years before, eucalyptus trees native to Australia had been planted throughout the Zoo, as part of a landscaping program that had the practical purpose of providing foods from varied native habitats for Zoo animals. Mrs. Benchley also had carefully studied the habits of the koalas, and she was able to convince Australian authorities that she could feed and nurture them. She had understood the near-reverence with which the Australian people regard the koala and finally wore down the opposition. Spurred finally by a Hollywood request for use of the koalas in a film, two pairs were shipped—first on loan, later as a gift—from the "children of Australia to the children of San Diego."

Today, when a koala finds itself caught in the crotch of a high tree, and firemen come to the Zoo to raise their ladders and get it down, you can tell from the smiling, intent faces of the bystanders that the San Diego Zoo is doing its job.

Sun Bear Forest (left) and Tiger River (below) are just two of the San Diego Zoo's newest animal exhibits that integrate plants and animals using the bioclimatic concept.

EPILOGUE

After reading this account of the San Diego Zoo's beginning, the obvious question is: what has happened since then? The complete telling of that story deserves another volume, but, briefly, it can be said that the Zoo has gone on to become everything Dr. Wegeforth ever dreamed.

Following the retirement of Mrs. Belle Benchley in 1953, Dr. Charles Schroeder became director of the Zoo in January of 1954. He was the Zoo's first leader with a scientific background in animal care. Dr. Schroeder received his doctor of veterinary medicine degree from Washington State University in 1929, and had initially been hired at the Zoo as a veterinarian/pathologist in 1932. He often recalled, however, that he would perform many other duties as well, like taking photographs to sell to visitors as postcards.

It was through Dr. Schroeder's vision and persistence that the San Diego Zoo's sister facility, the San Diego Wild Animal Park, came into existence and later opened to the public, in 1972. Here, in an 1,800-acre sanctuary, animals are allowed to roam freely in settings similar to their native habitats.

As director of the Zoo until 1972, Dr. Schroeder was also responsible for many other now well-known Zoo attractions, including the Skyfari aerial tramway, the Children's Zoo, and the moving sidewalk, or escalator. He further increased the Zoo's commitment to research and remodeled its hospital.

It was also during Dr. Schroeder's years as director that the local television show "Zoorama" was created, with its first airing in January 1955. Later syndicated nationally, the program brought the San Diego Zoo into the homes of millions of viewers across the nation.

The history of the Zoological Society of San Diego in recent times has been marked with an increased awareness of the role of zoos in our world. Under the able leadership of new directors and members of the board of trustees, the Society has become concerned with captive breeding and the conservation of wildlife. With the destruction of natural habitats worldwide and the resulting extinction of many species, it is now no longer possible to collect animals in the manner employed by Dr. Wegeforth and his colleagues. Zoo populations today must be self-sustaining and are being called upon to replenish wild populations.

It was through Dr. Charles Schroeder's persistence that the San Diego Zoo's sister facility, the San Diego Wild Animal Park (below) came into existence and later opened to the public in 1972.

EPILOGUE

Consequently, a number of conservation projects have been established both at the Zoo and Wild Animal Park, as well as elsewhere around the world. The first international conference on the role of zoos in conservation was hosted by the San Diego Zoo in 1966, during the celebration of the Zoo's 50th birthday. In addition, the Zoological Society presented its first conservation awards during that year.

Perhaps the best known of the Society's conservation projects has been the Center for Reproduction of Endangered Species, or CRES. Launched in 1975 as an intensive research effort to improve the health and breeding success of exotic animals, CRES is dedicated to its primary goal of helping endangered species of animals reproduce and survive. Some of the best known examples of CRES work have included gratifying reproductive successes with cheetahs, Indian and southern white rhinoceroses, and Przewalski's wild horses.

Keeping animals in enclosures that more closely resemble their native habitats has further helped these successes, as well as the overall health of the Zoo's animals. Building on ideas like those for Dr. Wegeforth's early lion grotto, which placed animals in a more natural setting rather than just a cage, the Zoo is presently committed to exhibits that use the bioclimatic concept. These enclosures integrate plants and animals from a specific region to provide both for the physical and emotional health of the animals and the education and entertainment of the public. Examples already completed are the Kopje, Tiger River, Sun Bear Forest, and Gorilla Tropics exhibits.

All of these accomplishments have more than fulfilled Dr. Wegeforth's dreams. The San Diego Zoo indeed "began with a roar," and that roar has turned into a record of achievement that can now be heard around the world.

Thomas L. Scharf
Editor, ZOONOOZ®

INDEX

Addison, Richard A., 115, **126**
Airedale dogs, 134
Alameda Street, 74
Alaskan fur seal, 163
Albert (elephant), 90
Albert (gorilla), **165,** 166, **167**
Alligator Canyon, **81**
Amazon, 66
American Museum of Natural History, 111
American Institute of Park Executives, 107
American Association of Zoological Parks and Aquariums, 108, 162, 168. *See also.* National Association of Zoological Executives.
Andrews, Charles N., 38
Annable, Fred, 38, 151
Arizona Railway, 44
Army Medical Board, 27
Army (San Diego Zoo keeper), 75, 76
Arnold (San Diego Zoo keeper), 155
Associated Press, 166
Auckland, New Zealand (zoo), 164
Australian Parliament, 169

B Mesa, 129
Baby Boo (elephant), 96
Baker, Dr. Fred, 71, 72, 86
Balboa Park, 24, 27, 59, 71, 72, 105, 125, 133
Baldwin, Carey, 156
Baltimore, 19, 20
Baltimore Health Department, 21
Baltimore Medical College, 22
Baltimore Northeastern Dispensary, 22
Barnes Brothers Circus, 94

Barnum and Bailey, 19
Bata (gorilla), **165,** 166. Also known as Oka.
Bean, Ed, 115
Bean, Robert, 115
Bear Grotto, **74,** 162
Benchley, Mrs. Belle, 22, 37, 59, **61,** 67, 115, 116, **116,** 129, 130, 139, 140, 144, 149, 150, 151, 153, 155, **156,** 164, 165, **165,** 166, **167,** 168, 169
Bering Sea, 163
Biological Research Institute and Zoological Hospital, 157
Blesbok antelope, 163
Bluebirds (organization), 155
Bong (cheetah), **133**
Boston Zoo, 101
Botany Bay koalas, **167**
Bouba (gorilla), **165,** 166. Also known as Lady Congo.
Boyle, Hal, 166
Brennan, Joe, 115
Bronx Zoo, 87
Brookfield Zoological Garden, 115
Brown, George, 84, 86
Brownie Scouts, 155
Bryan (camel), 122
Buck, Frank, 38, **39,** 90, 91, 93, 101, 114, 115
Buck, Mrs. Frank, **121**
Bum (condor), **99,** 147
Bureau of Fisheries, 162
Burger, Dr. T.O., 151
Burke, Lt. John, 153
Burlingame, Mrs. Dudley (Emily), 41, 160
Burnham, George, 30, **92**

175

Burridge, Admiral, 88
Butantan Snake Farm, 106

Caesar (bear), 72, 74, 75
Calcutta, 66
California Pacific International Exposition, 59
Camp Kearney, 129
Capps, Mayor, 72
Center for Reproduction of Endangered Species (CRES), 173
Central Park Zoo, 123, 124
Champlin, George, 77
Chesapeake Bay, 20
Chicago Zoo, 101
Children's Zoo, 171
Civil Service, 115
Cleveland Forest Reserve, 87
Coogan, Jackie, **55**
Cole Brothers Circus, 96
Colorado, 21
Commodore Hotel, 124
Consolidated Vultee Aircraft Corp., 144, 149
Cordtz, Mr., 80, 82
Coronado Islands, 156
Cotant, Charles L., 151, 157
County Jail, 22
Crandall, Captain Wesley C., 117, 151, 157, 160
Crandall, Lee, 162
Crosbie, Glen, **167**
Crouse, Lena P., 134, 148
Cuddles (koala), **126**
Culver (elephant), 94
Cuyamaca Club, 39, 49, 50

D-Day (giraffe), 154
Department of Agriculture, 41
Diablo (python), 34, **35,** 114

Dick (camel), 121
Ditmars, Dr. Raymond, 106, 123, 124
Dittoe, Georgia, **149,** 149
Doris (orangutan), 163
Dort, Ernest, 108
Dottie (llama), 155
Duck Island, 154
Duncan, Oklahoma, 31
Dutch East Indies, 64

Eastern Railway, 44
Ecuador, 64
Education Department, 134
Edwards, Harry, 91
Egypt (camel), **122**
Egyptian shoebills, 163
Elephant Barn, **97**
11th Street Canyon, 81
Elks Club, 84
Ellen Browning Scripps Foundation, 157, 160
Empress (elephant), 90, 92, 94, 95, 96, 97. *See also* Happy and Joy.
Escondido, 106
Evans, Victor, 107
Executive Committee, 113

F Canyon, 129
Faulconer, Tom, 24, 28, 115
Fern Canyon, 130
Fine Arts Gallery, 120
First National Trust and Savings Bank, 85
Founders Plaque, **70**
Fox, Sam, 117
France, W.B., 59, 125
Frye, Frank, 122
Fur Seal Commission, 162

Galápagos tortoises, 110
Galvin, Joe, 53, 67
Gallegos, J.N., 108

Georgie (chimp), 144, **147**
Gertie (tortoise), 158
Gill, Louis J., 28
Godwin, Percy, 107
Golden State Limited, 49
Gorilla Tropics, 173
Goura (pigeon), 151
Granger, Paul, 77
Granger, Rachel. *See* Wegeforth, Mrs. Harry M.
Granger, Ralph, 22
Granger Building, 22, 72
Gray, Gordon, 55, 151
Gregg, Dr., 71
Guadalupe Island, 61, 110, 111

Hagenbeck, Mr., 87
Hagenback Zoo, 147
Halsey, Admiral William F., 149, 152
Hamburg, Germany, 147
Hancock, Captain Allan, 28, 61, **63**, 64
Happy (elephant), 54, 92. *See also* Empress and Queenie.
Hari-Ki-Lash, 139
Harrower, Dr. Harry, 67
Harvester Building, **50,** 113, 117, 120
Harwell, Edalee Orcutt, 166, **167**
Hathaway, Mr., 89
Havemann, Richard, 147
Hazard, Roscoe, 105
Heck, Mr., 97
Heilbron, Carl, 76
Hendee, Jack, 86
Higgins, Shelley, 33
Hillyer, Curtis, 38
Hitler, Adolf, 162
Hollywood, 152
Holmes, Chris, 94
Hong Kong, 66
Hornaday, Dr., 87, 101
Hotel del Coronado, 57, 92

Howard, Ken, **150,** 155
Howard, Roy, 77
Humane Society of San Diego, 116, 117

Imperial Valley, 60
India, 66
Indian Village, 82
Ingram, Admiral, 155
International Harvester Company, 87
Irish (monkey), **99**

Japanese Tea Garden, 117
Jennings, Fred M., 22
Jensen, Holger and Helen, 141
Jensen, Otto, 84, 86, 141
Johnson (San Diego Zoo foreman), 129, 130
Johnson, James Hervey, 52
Johnson, Martin, 59, 60, 68, 139, 141
Johnson, Osa, **60,** 133, 141
Johnson, W. Templeton, 34
Jones, Albert J., 157
Joy (elephant), 54, 92. *See also* Empress and Queenie.
Junior San Diego Zoological Society, 77, 78

Kagu bird, 152
Kaufman, Mr., 75, 76
Kea birds, 163
Kelley, Dr. Arthur L., 160, 165
Kelly, Mike, 103
Kenya, 139, 152, 165
Kenyon, Karl W., 162
Kipling, Rudyard, 29
Kivu (gorilla), 139, 152
Klauber, Hugo, 35
Klauber, L.M., 106, 113, 123, 157, 168
Koch, Karl, 139
Koka, 108, 126
Kokok (organutan), 163
Kopje, 173
Kunzel, Fred, 151, 157

Lady Bear, **51**
Latimer, Hugh, 50
Laurel Street Bridge, 72
Leeper, Milton, 148
Lena II, 160
Lesser panda, **149**
Lewis, Fred, 28
Lint, K.C., 157, **159**, 163, 164
Lion Grotto, **102**, 103, **104**, 173
Little, Brown & Company, 147
Little Lotus (hippo), 151
Little Maya (elephant), 139
Lofty (giraffe), 141
London Zoo, 157
Look, 160
Los Angeles Zoo, 96
Lower Otay Dam, 59
Lucki (elephant), 139
Luehrman, A.D., 107

MacMullen, James, 88
MacRae, Colonel Milton, 124
MacRae Cages, **83**
Malaya, 154
Malmberg, J. Waldo, 151
Marie (walrus), **109**
Marine Mammal Hall, 111
Marston, George W., 34, 72, 77
Mbongo (gorilla), 59, 139, 140, 141, **143**, 144, 151, 152, 165, 166, 168
McArthur, Mary Elizabeth, 19
McGrew, Clarence, 59, 71, 88
McKinney, Dr. Frank, 160
McKinnon, Duncan, 78
McRorey, "Tex," **150**
Mercier, A.T., 28, 49
Merriwell, Frank, 166
Mexico City Museum, 111
Mickey (tapir), **148**
Middleton, Walter, 123

"The Mikado," 157
Mike (organutan), 118, 124, 158
Milwaukee Zoo, 115
Mirror Pool (Lagoon), **83,** 103, 108, 128
Monkey Mesa, 134
Monkey Quadrangle, **48, 49**
Moore, Byron, 151, 155
Moore, William, 81, 82
Mulford and Company, 106
Munich Zoo, 97
My Life in a Man-Made Jungle, **146,** 147
My Animal Babies, 154
My Friends, the Apes, 147

National Association of Zoological Executives, 57, 107. *See also* American Association of Zoological Parks and Aquariums.
National Zoological Park (Washington, D.C.), 107, 164
Natural History Society, 71, 120
Neuro-Surgical Institute of New York, 27
Nevada Building, 120, 127, 134
New Caledonia, 152
New York Zoological Society, 72, 101, 106, 123, 124, 152, 162
New Zealand, 163
Ngagi (gorilla), 59, 139, 141, **143,** 144, 151, 152, 165, 166, **167,** 168
Nile River, 163
Nolen Plan, 34
Northern Fur Seals, 162
Novak, Dr. Emil, 67

O'Connor, Jimmie, 144
O'Rourke, Patrick F., 39
O'Rourke, Mrs. Patrick, 119, 127
O'Rourke Building, 75, 120
Ocean Beach, 108
Olmstead, Lester T., 28, 117, 150

Open Forum, 127
Orinoco River, 66
Osborn, Fairfield, 152
Osborn, Rev. John B., 68
Otay Dam, 105

Pacific Coast Highway, 20
Panama-California International
 Exposition, 23, 24, 33, 71, 72, 78, 117, 120
Pape, Fred W., 107
Paramount Pictures, 160
Park Staduim, 34
Parks and Recreation, 107
Pasadena, 164
Pasteur Institute, 105
Patches (giraffe), 141
Pearl Harbor, 139, 140
Pepper Grove, 72, 78, 134
Perkins, C.B., 61, 64, 155
Pfefferkorn, M.C., 85, 86
Philadelphia Zoo, 162
Philippines, 64
Pichard, Doctor, 118
Pink Gopher Snake, 123-124
Plaza Hotel, 124
Point Loma, 106
Porterfield, W.H., 77, 88
Pribilof Islands, 162, 163
Prince (elephant), 94, 95, 96
Prince (lion), **104**
Puddles (hippo), **150**

Queenie (elephant), 90, 91, 92, 94. *See also* Happy and Joy.

Raffy (giraffe) 141, **145,** 154, 156
Raisbeck, Dr. Milton J., 67
Research Hospital, 117, 125, 155. *See also* San Diego Zoological Hospital.
Rhodes, Fred A., 127

Ring, Karl, **99**
Ringling, Charles, 89
Ringling, John, 89, 90, 91
Ringling Circus, 89, 122
Rogan, Nat, 45
Roosevelt School, 82
Rounan, Mr. and Mrs. John, 123
Ruby (hippo), 151
Russell, T.M, 74, 151
Russo, Joseph, 52
Rusty (giraffe), 157

S.S. Brazil, 66
Saigon, 66
Salton Sea, 60, 125
San Antonio Zoo, 164
San Diego Brownie Girls, 154
San Diego Embarcadero, 156
San Francisco, 150, 162
San Francisco Zoo, 156
San Diego Board of Park Commissioners, 72, 78, 80, 81, 115, 117, 127, 129, 160
San Diego City Board of Health, 32, 42
San Diego City Council, 33, 37, 42, 44, 52, 160
San Diego City Parks Department, 78, 103
San Diego City School Board, 117, 128
San Diego Civic Light Opera Association, 157
San Diego Elks Lodge, 87
San Diego Gas and Electric Company, 113
San Diego Hospital-Clinic, 42
"San Diego, I Love You," 152
San Diego Junior Zoological Society, 120, 127
San Diego Railway, 44
San Diego Soroptimist Club, 166
San Diego Sun, 42, 59, 77, 88, 125
San Diego Tribune, 59

San Diego Union, 24, 59, 68, 71, 88, 106, 120, 140
San Diego Wild Animal Park, 171, **172**
San Diego Zoological Hospital, 28, 129, 155. *See also* Research Hospital.
San Diego Zoological Society. *See also* Zoological Society of San Diego.
San Joaquin Valley, 144
San Luis Obispo, 115
The Saturday Evening Post, 160
Scar (camel), 122
Schwartz, Frank, 107
Science News Letter, 160
Scott, Maud, 113
Scripps, Ellen Browning, 46, 47, **47,** 57, 59, 75, 100, 101, 114
Scripps, Mrs. Robert P., 151
Scripps, John Paul, 124, 157
Sefton Jr., Joseph, 72, 77, 86
Sells Floto Circus, 88, 89
Sensenbrenner, Mr., 86
Schroeder, Dr. Charles, **122,** 171, **172**
Shanghai, 66
Shaw, Charles, 157, **159**
Shea, Mike, 52
Shelley, Freeman, 162
Shortridge, Samuel, 30, 92
Skyfari (aerial tram ride), 171
Smith, Charles, 94
Snooky (chimpanzee), 123
Snuggles (koala), **126**
Solomon Islands, 153
South America, 66
Southern Pacific Railroad, 49
Spreckels, John D., 30, 46, 54, 88, 91, 92, **92**
Spreckels Electric Company, 81
S.S. Brazil, 66
St. Louis Zoo, 162
St. Paul Island, 162
Standard Oil Building, 78, 119, 129
Star of India, 59

State of California, 52, 164
Stephens, Dr. Frank, 71, 101
Stott, Ken, Jr., 157, **158,** 162, **167**
Sullivan, Robert J., 151, 157, 168
Sun Bear Forest, **170,** 173
Susie (bear), 155
Sydney, Australia, 125
Sykes, E.G., 78

Talboy, Archie, 71
Taronga Park (zoo), 125
Taylor, Miss Sadie, 165, 166
Terry, General and Mrs. M.O., 82
Thompson, Dr. J.H., 71, 72, 78, 150
Thunder (zebra), 151
Tiger River, **170,** 173
Time, 152, 160
Titus, Horton L., 72
Tommy (elephant), 96
Tournament of Roses Parade, 164
Townsend Fur Seals, 111
Townsend, Dr. Charles, 110, **110**
Trefflich, Henry, 139, 165
Trinidad, 66
Trudy (tapir), 154
Turk (camel), 122
21st Army Infantry, 72, 82

Two Sisters, 156
Unitarian Church, 127
Universal Pictures, 152
University Club, 118
University of Maryland, 22, 67

Velero III, 61, **62,** 63, 66
Vierheller, George P., 107, 162
Virden, Ralph, 67, 96, 158
Volstead (camel), 122

Wadham, Mayor James E., 42
Warburton, Harry, 117

Wegefarth (Wegeforth), Ellen, 19
Wegefarth (Wegeforth), Emma, 19, 22
Wegefarth (Wegeforth), Conrad, 19
Wegeforth, Arthur, 19, 22, 66
Wegeforth, Charles, 20, 32
Wegeforth, Harry G., **169**
Wegeforth, Doctor Harry Milton: cartoon of, **138**; childhood of, 19-21; diary of, **65**; elephant and, **89**; founds Zoo, 71-72; Galápagos and, **62**; Hancock, Allan and, 61, **63**; Hollywood and, 77; marriage, 22; medical career, 41-44; medical school, 22; National Association of Zoo Executives, 57, **58**; office of, **84**; photos of, **4, 18, 20, 25, 26, 29, 38, 49, 67, 73**; python "Diablo" and, 34-35; sick tiger and, 40-41; Spreckels, John D. and, 91-92, **92**; travels of, 60-66; turtles and, 32; Wegeforth Bowl dedication, 30, **31**; ZOONOOZ start, 59
Wegeforth, Mrs. Harry M. (née Rachel Granger), **21, 67,** 141
Wegeforth, Lester, 32, **33, 67**

Wegeforth, Milton, 32, **67,** 68, 151, 157
Wegeforth, Paul, 19, 22, 23, **23**
Wegeforth Bowl, 30, **31,** 144, 155, 157
Wegeforth Day, 168
Wegeforth Memorial Education Building, 154
Weller, Mr. and Mrs. Frank, 123
Woman of the Year Award, 166
Woman's Club, 37
Wonderland Company, 76
Wonderland, Ocean Beach, 75
Works Progress Administration, 59, 140
World War II, 140
Wray, Daniel, 117

Yerkes, Dr. Robert M., 166

Zoo Education Department, 148
Zoological Society of San Diego, 28, 30, 31, 33, 37, 68, 71, 72, 74, 77, 78, 86, 89, 91, 96, 101, 107, 116, 127, 157, 168
ZOONOOZ, 59, 125, 130, **131, 132,** 151, 157
Zoorama, 171